A pastor in New York

A pastor in New York

The life and times of Spencer Houghton Cone

John Thornbury

 EVANGELICAL PRESS

EVANGELICAL PRESS
Faverdale North Industrial Estate, Darlington, DL3 0PH,
England

Evangelical Press USA
P. O. Box 825, Webster, New York 14580, USA

e-mail: sales@evangelicalpress.org

web: http://www.evangelicalpress.org

First published 2004

British Library Cataloguing in Publication Data available

ISBN 0 85234 512 7

Unless otherwise indicated scripture quotations in this publication are from the Authorized (King James) Version.

Front cover portrait provided by Ellen Van Bakergem of
Arlington, Va.
Artist: Anna Claypoole Peale

Printed in the United States of America.

Contents

List of illustrations

Foreword

God's gracious operation in building his church gives constant entertainment to the heavenly beings (Ephesians 3:10). His manifold wisdom continues to be displayed in how he has made the Gentiles fellow heirs of all the privileges and Messianic benefits promised through, and to, Israel. Those who were strangers and aliens, without hope, without God, without prophets, without covenant signs or promises, scattered abroad in the world, and hating one another, suddenly by one action of God in history and through the preaching of a battered and beaten apostle, who formerly despised them, were brought near. They received everything; rather, they had union with him who is everything — Christ: the wisdom, righteousness, holiness, and redemption from God. The seeming impossibility and absurdity of bringing into unity in one body such diverse, and hostile, peoples precisely express the joyful purpose of God.

Pandemonium becomes a symphony to God. Chaos takes form. One Lord has bought us, the Lord Jesus; one faith unites us to him, the disposition of mind and heart that affirms and feels all that is revealed to us concerning the reason for his incarnation, death and resurrection; only one baptism — that is, of believers by immersion, reflects that union of heart with the perfection of Christ's work; the work of the Holy Spirit alone has united us to Christ and his benefits; and we know the Father from whose person all unity, harmony, love, order, and relationship flow incessantly. The church embodies the earthly expression of the rich and infinitely glorious diversity within the unbroken and impenetrable unity of the triune God.

From the cacophony of disunited and hostile diversity emerges a singularity of purpose, passion and belief. This singularity expresses itself in an ever-increasing multiplicity of voices and gifts. Each of these diverse gifts moves energetically and intentionally towards a single goal and the expression of a single truth 'until we all attain to the unity of the faith and of the knowledge of the Son of God'. Unity of faith in no sense diminishes the singularity and individuality of the various personalities and unique expressions of the Spirit's variegated gifts to distinct members of the church. The power and beauty of such unity lies precisely in the fact that each of these gifts becomes a facet that contributes to, and is an expression of, the beauty of the whole.

Some interpretations of Baptist history today emphasize diversity and individuality with no observable focus on unity. The 'Faith' is seen as restrictive rather than expressive. Singularity in expression of belief about God and the doctrines of Christian revelation contradicts Christian freedom and diversity of gifts, so claims this ilk of historian. Messiness is in; harmony is out. To be Baptist means to embrace chaos. Any attempt at doctrinal clarity or unified focus in missionary endeavour destroys the genius of Baptist life, so the myth-writers insist.

Neither the historical construction nor the theological foundation for such an interpretation has warrant from the documents of Baptist history. Fiercely jealous for the purity of the local church, Baptists have embraced a view of the church that heightens confidence in the effectuality of the Spirit's work and diminishes, even scorns, the legitimacy of any human authority in the order or mission of the church. Neither civil government nor humanly-contrived church hierarchy may insert its authority into the life of the local church. Scripture functioning through the Spirit-endowed ministry suffices. But within each church and in the context of inter-church fellowship and mission a high degree of clarity about truth and discipline has operated. Clarity about work in the world and clarity about the message to be proclaimed have given unity and zeal to individual churches and the denomination as a whole.

The subject of this book is another testimony to this truth. Spencer Houghton Cone (1785-1855) is a microcosm of the unity and diversity that have characterized Baptist history. Uniquely gifted but single-minded with his brethren in the truth, Cone reflects the power and beauty of a lost generation of Baptist builders. His years of greatest power coincided with Baptist struggles for a national denominational programme of outreach and the encroaching denominational division over the sectional issue of slavery. With much historiographical attention given to the controversy generated by Alexander Campbell and the Anti-Mission Society movement and the tumultuous events that led to the departure of Baptists in the South from the still-young Triennial Convention, many Baptist ministers with consistent voices, creative energy, and faithful work have sunk out of historical sight. Spencer Cone, a powerful and godly influence in his day, is in that group.

Baptists believe in the necessity of *individual conversion*. Spencer Cone's confrontation in Scripture and in heart with the truth of his sinfulness drove him to Christ. Thornbury's narrative unfolds the simplicity as well as the relentless intensity of God's pursuit of this young man. Several months of struggle, conviction, and spiritual labour brought forth a joyful union with the completed work of Christ.

Baptists believe in a visible identification with Christ through baptism by immersion. Cone was plunged into a river in Maryland in February 1814, after breaking through twelve inches of ice. It was neither easy, comfortable, nor popular, but done in obedience to Christ.

Though consistent champions of *liberty of conscience*, Baptists have not isolated themselves from participation as *loyal citizens* of their country. Cone served in the military in the war of 1812, and was often in the heat of battle; he also served for a year as chaplain of the Congress. Cone's personal history shows how earnestly Baptists worked for religious liberty for all and yet how zealously they sought to be salt and light.

Baptists have given pre-eminence to the place of *preaching in the local church* as the highest call in Christian ministry and the most clearly established biblical means for evangelism and Christian growth. Cone delighted in his work in the church. He was effective as a pastor and powerful as a preacher. Thornbury's account of Cone's pulpit ministry and pastoral insight should encourage every Christian and every minister called by God. Salvation, sanctification, apertures into the glory of heaven fly to earth-bound sinners on the wings of Spirit-empowered preaching. Cone's remarkable gifts remind us that no human activity surpasses the glory of the preaching event. A young Thomas Armitage described Cone's preaching as characterized by 'simplicity of diction and pathos of spirit'. His voice at ready command was 'rich, powerful, and melodious, was vehement as the maddened storm — soft as the ascending strain from the lute — defiant as the bristling lion — mournful as the wooing dove — or startling as the martial trumpet'.

Baptists also have explored, in a variety of settings, the effectiveness of *associations* and *societies* in concentrating the strength of a large number of local churches for the sake of kingdom interests. Missionary work, both home and foreign, educational work, and publications have all benefited from the union of churches for these causes. Spencer Cone shows the kind of vigorous and conscientious involvement that challenged many Baptist leaders in the first half of the nineteenth century. These pioneering days in various benevolent enterprises brought about great victories, moulded heroic characters, and gave rise to tense confrontations. Again, through his narrative of Cone's involvement, Thornbury has not only let us see the particular exertions of a lion-hearted Baptist leader, but has opened a window on to the commitments of the larger denomination.

The vast majority of Baptists in America, North and South, from the seventeenth to the nineteenth centuries were Calvinists. Cone's convictions on these issues are unmistakable. He gloried in the sovereign grace of God and the omnipotent power, purpose, and effectuality of the Son's redemptive work and the Spirit's operations. His friend John L. Dagg, theologian of the South, asked him near his death if his views had changed on the doctrines of grace. Cone responded, 'Not a jot.' Thomas Armitage stated it clearly in the funeral sermon preached before his church, his family, the New York community, and many of his Baptist brethren: 'On this principle he was a Calvinist; a Calvinist of the old school, and felt no apology necessary for being so.'

This theological position did not merely eke out a life in the dark corners of a theological attic, but thrived in the bright light of open confession and pulpit oratory. Not only did he preach 'the distinctive doctrines of that school,' like other Baptists of his time, Cone expressed his theology as a strong *confessionalist.* His move to Oliver Street Baptist Church in New York was not done before he presented to them the 'leading tenets of that ministry which I profess to have received of the Lord Jesus.' A clear and precise abstract of the orthodox, evangelical, Calvinism of Baptists including 'personal and unconditional election; [the special relationship of Christ's atonement] to the sins of his people; ...the imputed righteousness of Christ alone ...effectual calling, ...perseverance of the saints; believers baptism by immersion only; ...the obligation of every intelligent creature to love God supremely' and other biblical doctrines constituted his personal confession. That confession served as the seedbed for the confession that he led the First Baptist Church of

New York to adopt when he became pastor there in 1841. The twenty-article confession of faith, along with a church covenant, was unanimously adopted and published with an affirmation of the appropriateness of the practice: 'We deem it expedient and proper to publish the Summary of our Faith and Articles of our Church Covenant.'

While Cone had a catholic spirit and cultivated friendships with gospel-loving Christians of all denominations, he believed strongly in the *peculiar distinctives of Baptists*. He read widely and mastered such non-Baptist writers as Thomas Scott, Matthew Henry, Jonathan Edwards, John Owen, and John Calvin. His benefits from them were great but did not dissuade him from the biblical purity of distinguishing Baptist doctrine. From the time of his conversion till the day of his death, he believed that obedience to the clear commands of Jesus Christ made necessary the practice of baptism of believers only, and that by immersion. He even believed that Scripture translation should reflect this. His intimate involvement in the American and Foreign Bible Society and the American Bible Union were functions of this very principle expressed in the motto — The Bible Translated.

John Thornbury has enriched the coffers of Baptist biography by this offering of an edifying and sympathetic biography of Spencer Cone. An almost forgotten name a sesquicentennial after his death, during his life none could think of the Baptists without picturing Cone as their paradigm. Sit back for an easy, edifying and important read. When you have finished you will be sorry that you missed him in this life and will not wonder why Cathcart's *Baptist Encyclopedia* closes its biography of Cone with the following synopsis:

> For many years, Dr Cone was the most active Baptist minister
> in the United States, and the most popular clergyman in
> America. He was known and venerated everywhere all over

this broad land. In his own denomination he held every position of honor which his brethren could give him, and outside of it men loved to recognize his worth. He had quick perceptions, a ready address, a silvery voice, impassioned eloquence, and deep-toned piety; throngs attended his church, and multitudes lamented his death. He entered the heavenly rest 28 August 1855.

Dr Tom J. Nettles
Professor of Historical Theology
Southern Baptist Seminary,
Louisville,
Kentucky,
USA

Preface

I live about ninety miles from Gettysburg, Pennsylvania, where nearly one hundred and fifty years ago the decisive battle in the great struggle known as the Civil War was fought. I never tire of going there and driving around, hearing, thinking, and learning about the awesome events that transpired on those wooded hills and rolling pastures.

Especially impressive are the memorials to the courageous men in grey and blue who gave there the utmost of their devotion to their cause. Virtually all the states which sent their sons into the fury of battle have erected monuments in their honour. Great guns still point their muzzles towards the sky, though no enemy now opposes them.

Bronze statues stand there representing the brave men who fought, and in some cases, died for what they believed. In sunshine and in rain, in spring, summer, autumn and winter, they watch in motionless vigil over the green pastures where so much blood was shed. George Gordon Meade, mounted on his bronze steed, stares across the stone wall where his Yankee men faced the fury of the soldiers from the South. And Robert E. Lee, indomitable general who led the Southern armies, several hundred yards away faces him, sentenced, I have often thought, to a perpetual misery, as he must in eyes of metal for ever behold the scene of the slaughter of his army.

Jesus Christ once said that the sons of this world are more shrewd in their generation than the 'sons of light'. Men and women whose friends and relatives lived and died in conflicts like the Civil War make sure that there is proper remembrance of what they did. Much time and much expense, rightly and wisely I might add, are given to ensure that posterity never forgets their exploits. Great statues and inscriptions on marble tell to passers-by of their courage and dedication. Tens of thousands of volumes describe in amazing detail how these men of war planned, charged, retreated, shot, suffered, and often fell in agonizing death to the ground under their feet.

But Christians, whether through ignorance, selfishness, or perhaps simply carnal indifference, often allow their departed heroes to perish unremembered. The writers of Scripture did not. The lives and deeds of the people of God who lived in Bible days are faithfully recorded by those who were inspired by the Holy Spirit to write them down. Some like Abraham, Moses, Samuel, David, Elijah, Peter and Paul are given a lot of space and attention. Others are simply noted in passing, but it is interesting to ponder the fact that God, who in his infinite wisdom gave us his Word, left their names in Holy Writ.

This book gives me an opportunity to rediscover and present to our generation the life of a wonderful man of God, who has suffered an undeserved anonymity: Spencer Houghton Cone. Here is a story about a marvellous conversion, the overcoming of hardships through faith, the power of great preaching, and the influence of a godly life. His story shows the prominent place that the Doctrines of Grace should have in the history and life of Baptists in America. In the following pages, I seek to commemorate his ministry, and also as a not insignificant addendum, the life of the wonderful woman to whom he was married. Together they worshipped, laboured, sacrificed and died. They were beautiful examples of perseverance in the face of hardship and trial, devotion to the gospel, zeal for truth, and compassion for the people of their own day.

The primary source materials on the life of Cone are Sprague's *Annals of the American Pulpit*, with its article on Cone; several articles and essays of our subject written as circular letters of the New York Baptist Association; William Cathcart's *Baptist Encyclopedia*, Baptist histories by Thomas Armitage and Robert Torbet; Cone's funeral oration by Armitage (running to some fifty-six pages); but especially the standard biography, *Some Account of the Life of Spencer Houghton Cone, A Baptist Preacher in America*, written by his sons Edward and Spencer Wallace. This volume, with its first-hand account of Cone's life by members of his family, contains a lot of correspondence from friends and associates such as John L. Dagg, Baron Stow and Francis Wayland. These letters written to the authors give important independent support to the views of Cone's sons on their father's gifts and ministry.

For the secular historian, there may be something of interest here, but probably not much. For one interested merely in politics, or philosophy, or geography, or genealogy, or for the leisure reader who is only looking for entertainment, this book will no doubt seem worthless. But for a child of God, particularly one devoted to the gospel of the grace of God, the following pages will be a source of inspiration, faith and encouragement. I hope so. And now, as the old writers used to say, 'Courteous reader', open these pages, read, reflect, and thank God for the testimony of some saints who, though long dead, live on through the legacy of their teachings and experiences in the journey of life.

What you are about to read is not fiction; it is sober history. It tells of what actually happened, not what exists solely in the fevered fantasies and imaginations of pious dreamers. There are no tales here of weeping statues, healings by contact with the bones of dead saints, or appearances of heavenly apparitions, but there are true stories of courage and faith. Such should nourish your spirit.

1.

Birth and childhood

In 1785 England and the United States were finally at peace because three years previously in the Treaty of Paris America's independence had been recognized. It would not be long before the representatives of the various colonies would be meeting in Philadelphia to frame a constitution. The winds of religious liberty, which Baptists and other groups had desired for so long, were beginning to blow. James Madison who, perhaps as much as anyone, championed the concept of unlimited political and religious freedom, abolished all religious tests in Virginia through his Religious Freedoms Act. From Vermont to Georgia, from the shores of New Jersey to the untamed wilderness of Kentucky, Americans of all religious and ethnic backgrounds were beginning to 'dream dreams and see visions' of a new land of incredible opportunity and prosperity.

On 30 April 1785, not far from the stately halls of Princeton College in New Jersey, Alice Cone, wife of a revolutionary war veteran, Conant Cone, gave birth to a baby boy who would grow up to be an eminent Christian and powerful preacher of the gospel of Jesus Christ. He was named Spencer Houghton, the middle name taken from the family of Alice who was the daughter of Colonel Joab and Catherine Houghton.

Spencer Cone came from noble stock, and this helps to explain his moral and theological fibre. The paternal ancestor of Conant Cone was a Puritan named Roger Conant who came

to Massachusetts in 1620, one of the thousands who were fleeing the persecution in England. He, along with a minister from
Dorchester, England, attempted to found a settlement at Cape
Ann. Unfortunately this venture failed. But Conant was a man
of strong ambition, determination and resilience. After paying
off those who had been employed in the scheme (for he was
the chief agent), he and three others went to Salem, resolved
that there they would make a stand for the principles in which
they believed.

Like so many of the early settlers of Massachusetts, the
descendants of Roger Conant eventually pushed forward into
the river valley of Connecticut. The Conant family chose East
Haddam as its location, and settled there to establish a home.
Here three or four generations away from the original emigrant
Conant, the father of Spencer Houghton was born — named
after his courageous ancestor.

His maternal grandparents had experienced in their own
personal history the need for liberation from the tyranny of an
intolerant religious system. Catherine Houghton was the child
of one of the early Huguenot refugees and both of her parents
were of the 'stern old French Calvinists', who had weathered
the storms of Catholic persecution in the days of King Louis
XIV. These believers had steadfastly held to their faith in the
Cevennes mountains, even while suffering terrible trials and
hardships. They were among the first emigrants to the new world
who believed in the priesthood of believers and freedom of
conscience. The Huguenots were fiercely independent in their
convictions not only with respect to political liberties but religious ones as well. They were opposed to dictatorial church
hierarchies and stood bravely against all government intrusion
into the spiritual concerns of individuals.

Conant Cone left East Haddam, Connecticut, as a young
man and moved to Hunderdon county in New Jersey where he
became deeply involved in the disputes between the American
colonists and the British government. Here he met and became

associated with Joab Houghton, his future father-in-law, who had become an assembly man in the local government. Dissatisfaction with the Royal government in New Jersey had led to the organization of the Provincial Congress of that colony in 1776. After the Declaration of Independence, New Jersey proceeded to organize a militia to join Washington's army which was mustering its forces for the defence of the new nation. Joab Houghton was one of the first men to be appointed as an officer in the colonial army. The citizens of Hunderdon county elected him as a member of the Assembly when a state government was organized in New Jersey.

Houghton was a Baptist and attended the Baptist church at Hopewell in Hunderdon County. It was while he was worshipping in the old Hopewell Baptist Church that a messenger whispered to him the news about the battle of Lexington, the first hostilities that would ignite the revolutionary war. Joab sat quietly through the service, but as soon as the worshippers were dismissed he stood on a great stone block outside the church and called the people together for an important announcement. What message did their friend and neighbour, Joab Houghton, have to deliver to them just after a season of prayer, singing and listening to a gospel message? What they heard that day saddened their hearts and turned their joyful mood into one of deep solemnity. They were told how their compatriots near Boston had been shot down in cold blood by the Red Coats and about the turmoil that had followed. Looking upon the crowd of Baptists that day, who stood in death-like silence, he said, 'Men of New Jersey, the Red Coats are murdering our brethren of New England! Who follows me to Boston?' Every man who had attended the worship service stepped forward and volunteered to serve. 'There was not a coward nor a traitor in old Hopewell meeting house that day.'[1]

Conant Cone and the daughter of the fearless leader who summoned the men for war after the service attended that same Hopewell church and were baptized there as well. With the land he loved in imminent peril Conant Cone joined Joab Houghton and enlisted as a soldier in the colonial army, where he served bravely and at considerable cost. He had the unique privilege of working directly under George Washington himself and was a guide to the great General during some of his critical military manoeuvres in New Jersey. Owing to the special situation he was in, he got to know the commander-in-chief personally and developed a deep love and veneration for him.

After the war Washington was given the distinguished title of 'Father of his Country'. An interesting and auspicious event took place after the war when the lives of Washington and the Cone family intersected for a brief moment. On one occasion the General was taking one of his well-known triumphal tours through a part of the Middle States, where he received the acclamations and praise everywhere of the huge crowds which thronged the highways to see the conquering hero. The Cone family was fortunate enough to be by the roadside when one such victorious procession passed by, with Washington leading the way. Conant took in his arms his baby boy and went out to meet his General for whom he had served so faithfully. Recognizing immediately his valuable aide who had borne with him the heat and fury of many battles, Washington took the baby in his arms, kissed him and blessed him. That baby boy was the first of six children: Spencer Houghton. What a benediction for the person who would some day move the multitudes with his preaching! Who can doubt that the prayer of Washington was one of the instruments of God's special calling for the one he had chosen?

Spencer grew up in a little old-fashioned frame house not far from Princeton College. The most important formative influence in his childhood was his mother, who was a bright, energetic woman of indomitable spirit. More importantly she was a devout believer who brought her children up to fear God, love freedom, and bathed her pillows at night in tears of compassion for their conversion to God. He was taught at his mother's knee love for the Bible, dedication to strict principles of integrity in all his dealings with men, and fierce loyalty to his country. From his father and grandfather he heard first hand stories of the thrilling events of the revolutionary war. His first lessons in life were learned from the celebrated heroes of the colonial army, the brave veterans of Bunker Hill, Saratoga and Yorktown. Long before he could take a gun or ride a horse an ambition was instilled in him to serve his country in any way he could. In America's next war he had just such an opportunity.

But the glory, the honour and the soul-stirring traditions which formed the background of his family circle had a dark side as well. The wounds he had received in battle and the privations the war had brought upon him had left his father a broken man. Conant Cone had sacrificed everything for the defence of his country, and as a result his economic resources were nearly exhausted. Only through the diligence and frugality of a noble woman was he able to eke out a bare existence for his growing family. In fact, the dark memories of the late military struggle, his own shattered physical health and the pressures of life generally drove the man into deep depression. Eventually his mental state became such that he was unable to support his family at all, and the responsibility fell upon his eldest son.

Spencer, inspired by the example of his mother and being naturally precocious, took to his studies with great zeal. Encouraged by her he studied Greek, Latin and mathematics till he became proficient in these and other disciplines. He collected a library of classical literature and cultivated a remarkable memory. While still a teenager he became conversant with the writings of Cicero, Seneca and Homer and could quote extracts from them for the rest of his life. He entered Princeton College at the age of twelve and, in spite of many distractions and responsibilities at home, he distinguished himself academically. Among his classmates were James Fennimore Cooper, the novelist, and John Forsythe, who later became Secretary of the United States Treasury. But the unfortunate condition of his father proved to be a final blow to his college career.

When Spencer Cone was only fourteen years of age, in the midst of his promising career as a student at Princeton, the mind of his father gave way. Conant was a courageous soldier, a warm-hearted friend to man and a loving father, but in matters financial he was a colossal failure. Poverty, bankruptcy and even starvation stared him in the face. He was physically unable to work and too proud to beg. The stress was too much for him. With the head of the Cone household thus incapacitated, the call of hearth and home came to the Princeton student. A defenceless mother, a stricken father, and four small children were being reduced to destitution. Could he, would he put behind him his own ambitions and assume the burden of supporting his family? Spencer never hesitated. He left behind Nassau hall and said to his mother, 'Mother, you have worked to feed me while I got an education and now, with God's blessing, my education shall feed you.'

2.

Actor

Spencer Houghton Cone had to grow up fast. At the age of fourteen when most youth his age were mingling household chores with games, fishing, and other forms of fun and frolic, he was assuming the bread-winning responsibilities for a family of eight, including himself. But how could he make a living for them? In God's providence a local doctor kept a school thirty miles away at Basking Ridge and advertised for an assistant. Did he stand a chance of being hired? His threadbare clothes, elbows totally worn thin would not recommend him for such a position. His mother had a beautiful red cloak which she decided to rip apart and make into a coat for him, all the while praying fervently that God would bless her child with a job to help them through their time of destitution. Spencer went for the interview, wearing his new coat dyed brown, full of hope and anticipation. But a bitter disappointment awaited. After a thirty mile walk he was to learn that the day before a teacher had been secured. And so with a heavy heart he made his way back home to break the dreadful news to his mother.

But the Lord had not forgotten him. In September of the year 1810 he was able to secure a job as a Latin teacher at the Princeton Academy much nearer home. He had a job, but, in his own words, 'It barely kept us alive.' These were days of self-denial, poverty and debt which he always remembered as a period of great disappointment, almost despair. A sovereign God had called upon the youth to drink deeply from the cup of bitterness. His poor father too was out of his mind half the time. They tried to hospitalize him in Philadelphia, but a person who did not reside in Pennsylvania could be taken only when a sum of money was put up for security. This the pathetic family could not manage. These were dark moments in their lives, but moments which God was using in the life of Spencer to train him for battles against the forces of spiritual darkness which he would encounter in later life.

The youthful teacher was, however, demonstrating his mettle as a leader and as a teacher during these days. He had shown himself to be studious, scrupulous, and very gifted as an instructor. Although forced by providential necessity to pull a heavy load against many contrary winds, he was growing in strength and confidence. His position at the Princeton Academy had prepared him for an excellent opportunity to become the headmaster of a district school at Burlington, a town on the Delaware River near Philadelphia. This position, which came to him as a new century was dawning, was a considerable advance.

The school was in a very prosperous and wealthy section of New Jersey. The inhabitants were for the most part either Quakers or descendants of Quakers, whose industry and thrift had given them a place of prominence as citizens. Very little of the peculiarities of Quaker sternness remained at this time; instead the citizens of Burlington country were a lively and worldly generation who delighted in their fine horses, fat cattle and pleasurable social activities. In a short time Spencer gained much popularity among them, and he soon became a part of the inner circle of the community. His salary was doubled and he was given free board and lodging. Now he was able to lift his family out of their abject poverty and provide for them as he had long wished.

Soon other avenues of advancement came. Before long he attracted the attention of Dr Abercrombie, principal of the Chief

Academy at Philadelphia, who recognized his ability immediately. He accepted an invitation to be his assistant, which enabled him to move the whole family to Philadelphia. But living expenses in the great city were such that even a good job was not sufficient to make ends meet, so he entertained the ambition of entering the practice of law. With this in mind he took a job as a law clerk to supplement his salary and to help to train him for the legal profession. During the daylight hours he was a teacher, and at night he pored over the writings of Coke and Blackstone and copied documents from the law office. It was too much. The uninterrupted pressures of teaching, studying and working with legal documents, without any breaks for recreation or relaxation, began to take a toll on his health. He lost his appetite, became anaemic and began to have pains in his chest. Still he pressed on.

What should he do? An Episcopal bishop encouraged him to enter the priesthood, promising him that he would have a comfortable career and would get adequate help for his theological training. The bishop assured him that he had all the assets necessary to be a powerful preacher: a marvellous voice, agile mind and winning personality. But, though not a believer at the time, he knew even then that only a call from God could warrant entrance into the profession of the ministry. The cleric then recommended what turned out to be a pivotal course of action. 'If you will not be a priest,' he concluded, 'then you should be an actor.' The advice was well intentioned, but from the standpoint of the Puritan-Baptist tradition from which he descended, it was dangerous.

The theatre in Spencer Cone's day, as indeed still is the case among many serious Christians, was looked upon as something totally incompatible with a Christian profession. No Baptist in good standing with the regular Baptist churches would frequent the stage, where in the context of fictitious drama the world was exhibited as it is, not as it should be. The theatre was anathema to the Puritan conscience and to be an actor was equivalent to choosing gambling or theft as a trade.

Spencer knew, as did many others, that his disposition made him a natural for the stage. Already he had seen how he could sway a class with his masterly use of language. The traumas of his past life, the brutal experiences with many kinds of people, as well as the broadening of his intellectual horizons, had put him in touch with the depths of human emotion. But should he turn in this direction? His mother opposed it. His conscience, based on principles long cherished by his family and ingrained in him from childhood, tugged against him. Still the grinding poverty he had known, the insufferable load he had assumed as a breadwinner, and the seemingly limitless vistas of fame and fortune that opened up through this once-in-a-lifetime opportunity were too much. And so in 1805 he joined a theatrical company.

In the heart of Philadelphia in the early nineteen hundreds was the Chestnut Street Theatre, which was then at the zenith of its glory. Some of the most talented performers in America were a part of it, and great crowds flocked to witness the most exciting new plays, as well as the classical productions of the past. Although a mere boy with limited experience and no social rank to propel him into such a prestigious position, Spencer Cone became a spectacular success from the start. His first dramatic role was to play Achmet in a play about Mahomet, and his effort was greeted with immediate acclaim. With his scruples adequately suppressed, he gave himself with unfettered ardour to the study of his trade. He read everything he could get his hands on that would enhance his skill as an actor. He studied the best models, and especially he became enamoured with the Garrick school which strove through 'pantomimic adaptation' to use the human voice and gestures to arouse maximum emotional response from the audiences.

Spencer Cone's thespian star rose quickly. For five years he performed in the most prestigious theatres, primarily in the region of Philadelphia, Baltimore and Washington D.C. The highest ranks of the political and social circles of these great cities came to hear him, and his 'fan club', speaking in modern terms, grew rapidly. His name became a household word particularly in Philadelphia. Before he had reached the age of twenty-five, the erstwhile farm boy, who in recent memory had walked a dusty road in New Jersey in his mother's shawl to rescue a family from destitution, was now the toast of the town.

But in the midst of all this popularity and public acclaim there was a deep-seated emptiness within. He began to see what a shallow, superficial place the stage was, with all its pretentious glamour and glory. He saw what the power of speech and acting could do to inflame the passions of men and even stir them to noble deeds of service to their fellow man. But, when all was said and done, it was only pretence. The world of fiction and fantasy slowly lost its appeal. At last his thoughts began to run like this: 'How much nobler and more worthy of an American it would be to live the reality of heroic virtue — to act instead of mimicking the deeds of greatness. I will be a living worker in the world — I will play no more.'[1]

Of course, Spencer's prominence as an actor caused him to be noticed by all sectors of society. One of those who frequented his productions was Sally Morrell, the daughter of Mary Morrell, who had been married to a wealthy citizen of Philadelphia, a man named Robert. He was a seaman and had served with distinction during the revolutionary war. Mary had a brother named Chandler Price who was an eminent merchant not only well disposed financially but also prominent in the city. After her father's death Sally went to live with him. The Price household was the centre of the social activities of the upper classes of Philadelphia. Here she enjoyed all the opportunity which the high station of her uncle afforded, including the meeting of eminent citizens. She was beautiful, cultured and ambitious, accustomed to the finest of clothing and trained in the manners and fashions of the rich.

The paths of Mary Morrell and Spencer Cone crossed at numerous public places which provided amusement for the upper classes: the theatre, the dance hall and the race course. Admiration soon grew to fondness on her part, and finally her heart was smitten by a deep love for him. Her uncle was outraged at the attention she was giving to one whom he considered unworthy of her status. But in the end all his resistance, his counsels and warnings only served to fan the flame of affection. They were eventually engaged and married, and the letters from Spencer to Mary which remain tell us much about the character of the man she would accompany to the Baptist ministry. She proved to be a worthy helpmate in every way, willing, when duty eventually called, to abandon the gay and elegant society she had enjoyed to take up the cause of the gospel.

In 1810 Spencer's resolve to abandon the stage strengthened and he confessed that his profession was becoming more and more disgusting to him. At this time his interests turned to military science, for patriotism had been ingrained in him from childhood. The winds of war were gathering again and American vessels were increasingly being harassed on the Atlantic. To him the cause of America symbolized all that was politically and morally right. He knew that in the United States for the first time in history political and spiritual freedom had an opportunity to flourish. As far as he was concerned any threat to the United States was a menace to that which was the most noble and best. It was inevitable, then, that when hostilities broke out between Great Britain and America, he would enlist as a soldier and serve in any capacity possible.

3.

Conversion

God had his hands on this teacher turned actor from New Jersey. His destiny was not to be a rustic farmer in the fields of his native state, a brilliant educator in the academies of Philadelphia, nor a successful actor thrilling the crowds in the theatres of Baltimore, nor even a military genius, though he had the mind and skills for all of these. Like Paul he was separated from his mother's womb to preach the gospel. The basic elements of that gospel were familiar to him, though he had never seriously sought the Lord while his mid-twenties passed by. He had heard God's call to trust in Jesus in the old Hopewell meeting house even as a child. He recalled in later life one message which had particularly moved his heart. Rev. James McLaughlin preached a sermon which Spencer heard when he was only eight, at a time when he was spending a few months with his grandfather Houghton. The text was Jeremiah 8:22: 'Is there no balm in Gilead; is there no physician there?' This sermon embedded in its message a theology he never forgot.

He remembered clearly the outline. Point one was 'total depravity'. Point two was 'universal condemnation'. Point three was 'salvation alone by the balm of Gilead — the blood of the Lamb'. The sermon so affected him that for months he could not go to sleep without saying the Lord's prayer or some other form of prayer taught him by his mother. But these thoughts wore off and were drowned in childish play.

About two years later he went with his mother to hear a sermon by the great Presbyterian minister Ashbel Green of Philadelphia. He preached powerfully from John 1:29: 'Behold the Lamb of God, which taketh away the sin of the world.' Again he was convicted of sin and of his need of divine grace. He strove to improve his life, but such efforts were only self-induced, without seeking divine assistance. Once again these impressions proved to be like the morning cloud, passing away as soon as they came. Such messages, however, lodged in his heart and made him ever conscious of the reality of the Creator and the basic truths of the Christian faith. Even during his meteoric rise to fame as an actor, with all its temptations and follies, the truths he had learned as a child kept him from the greater evils of many of the others with whom he consorted.

But in 1813, one year into the war with England, his life took a dramatic turn for the better as far as his spiritual state was concerned. A year earlier he had secured, along with his brother-in-law John Norvell of Kentucky, ownership of the *Baltimore Whig*, a newspaper. In the midst of the war he sustained with all might the cause of the Madison administration, while at the same time commanding the Baltimore Union Artillery Company. His mind was totally occupied with politics and war; the state of his soul seldom concerned him.

But in November as he sat at his breakfast table reading a newspaper he saw, among other things, that there was a book sale at a local auction. Curious as to what volumes might be available (the subjects that most interested him at that time would have been history, politics and military strategy), he went to see for himself. The book which, in God's good design, immediately caught his attention was one he had read when at Princeton on the life of John Newton. He remembered as clearly as if he had read it yesterday God's amazing grace in the life of the old slave trader. He promised the owner that he would be back later to purchase the book and left to walk the city streets.

It was when he was walking to his office, even while in the middle of the street, that an inner voice spoke to him, saying, 'This is your last warning.' It came as powerfully as the 'sound of many waters'. He felt that the Almighty was holding him in his hand, and a sense of accountability to him overwhelmed him. 'I trembled as an aspen leaf,' he said. The sermons of McLaughlin and Green came back to him with renewed freshness and clarity. It seemed that the day of doom had come for him. He was so shaken that when he took down the day-book to record the new advertisements, his hand trembled so that he could not write. He placed the book back on the shelf.

Unable to pursue his normal business activities he went out on to South Street and walked up and down Market till the evening meal trying to drown out, if possible, his alarming thoughts. 'This is your last warning,' the voice echoed and re-echoed, as if he were soon to be summonsed to the Supreme Judge. He sought to conceal his thoughts from his wife during the evening, and as the hour for the sale of the book approached he was there in haste to purchase it. Once again he read the thrilling story of Newton's conversion and was unable to put it down before going to bed. He became aware of some similarities between his life and Newton's. Like him he had been brought up in a Christian home, like him he had strayed far from the path of godliness, and like him he had ignored many warnings. But, hopefully, God had preserved him from the disasters which could have befallen him.

Laying aside the volume he had purchased, Spencer began to study the Bible in earnest. He was determined to find out, if possible, how one could be saved from sin and hell. He read different portions of the Old Testament, particularly the Psalms, and read the New Testament through twenty times. Especially he studied the Gospel of John and the Epistle to the Romans. So absorbed in the subject of religion was he that he found it difficult to attend to domestic and business duties. His wife, whom he loved dearly, thought he was losing his mind. He realized now for the first time that it would yield him nothing if he gained the whole world but lost his soul.

He started going to church hoping to find some light to shine on his path. 'What must I do to be saved?' was the question he asked day and night. He listened to many ministers but none of them showed clearly how a poor sinner could find peace with God. One evening, after his family had retired, he went into a vacant watchtower and paced back and forth in great agony of mind. He thought of Hezekiah who turned his face to the wall when the cruel armies of Sennacherib had invested Jerusalem, so he did the same. He cried to God for mercy. An impression that he would have to suffer this mental distress for as long as he had lived in neglect of his Creator seized him. But this seemed a most welcome bargain. 'Yes, dear Lord,' he cried out, 'a thousand years of such anguish as I now feel, if I may only be saved at last.'

For a considerable period he alternated between reading the Bible and returning to the recesses of the garret where he pleaded with God to save his poor lost soul. This went on for several days. Then one night, the Lord used the symbolism of Noah's ark to show him the true way of redemption. He saw in his mind the awful Flood that swept away the guilty generation of Noah's day, but he saw also how Noah and his family were saved. Just as God invited this ancient group into the great vessel for safety and shut the door, so he perceived that God had provided an ark of safety for him. That ark was Christ. Long afterwards as a mature minister, he recalled this momentous time:

> I saw distinctly that in Christ alone I must be saved, if saved at all; and the view I, at that moment, had of God's method of saving sinners, I do still most heartily entertain, after thirty years' experience of his love. That was Saturday night, and that night I slept more sweetly than I had done for many weeks.

Before daylight on Lord's day morning I awoke, and went down stairs quietly, made a fire in the front parlor, and threw open the window-shutters, and as soon as I could see, commenced reading the New Testament. I opened to the thirteenth chapter of John and came to where Peter said, 'Thou shalt never wash my feet.' Jesus answered him, 'If I wash thee not, thou hast no part with me.' Simon saith to him, 'Lord not my feet only, but also my hands and my head.' At that moment my heart seemed to melt. I felt as if plunged into a bath of blood divine — I was cleansed from head to foot — guilt and apprehension of punishment were both put away; tears of gratitude gushed from my eyes in copious streams; the fire in the grate shone on the paper upon the wall, and the room was full of light; I fell upon the hearth-rug, on my face, at the feet of Jesus, and wept and gave thanks; my sins, which were many were all forgiven, and a peace of mind succeeded which passeth understanding. Bless the Lord, O my soul! From that hour to the present, a doubt of my calling and election of God has never crossed my mind.[1]

His first impulse was to obey the Lord in the ordinance of believer's baptism. He had no question whatsoever as to the proper way to be baptized. He had not conferred with flesh and blood, and indeed there was no need to do so. He went to the pastor of the First Baptist Church of Baltimore, Lewis Richards, and asked if he could be baptized. After a couple of interviews and a session in which he gave his testimony to sixty or so members of the church, he was approved. On Saturday morning, 14 February 1814 he was baptized in the Patapsco River by pastor Richards. The water was reached for this ceremony only after twelve inches of ice had been cut. In fact, the people were able to walk up to the spot where the elderly minister, who performed this service even though he was crippled with rheumatism, dropped Spencer Cone beneath the bone-chilling waters. It was a day never to be forgotten by any: the candidate, the pastor and the devout people who watched it all.

Spencer's wife was totally baffled by all that was happening
to him. She had been brought up as a strict Episcopalian of a
high liturgical order. A thorough-going formalist in so far as she
had any religious convictions, she had been taught that all dis-
senters from the Church of England were dangerous rebels
against all truth and goodness. It is no wonder that she was
alarmed and confused when her husband began to spend time
alone with God every day in prayer and Bible reading. How
could her beloved husband, the very embodiment of merri-
ment and wit, full of the gusto of life, capable of holding multitudes spellbound with his powerful impersonations on the stage,
suddenly become a morose penitent? And then to crown it all,
he had decided to join what she considered to be the most
extreme of the sects, the straight-laced Baptists who frowned
on all the gaieties she enjoyed: the dance hall, the race course
and the theatre.

She loved him so dearly that she could not and would not
allow any interruption in their marital bliss because of his religious change, but secretly she seethed with anger and disgust.
But whatever her reservations or private opinions, being a
woman of character she knew her duty. Stifling, restrictive and
narrow as it was in her eyes, she would now take her place
beside him in the simple Baptist worship services. She could
now no longer parade in the richly ornamented cathedrals of
her own church but must sit in the dull and dismal chapels of
the Baptists. It was an awful trial to her.

Too proud to do so openly, she began to steal a furtive glance
at the Book that had transformed her husband. His patience
and tenderness softened any alienation that may have grown
up between them, and carefully and gently he led her along as
she too began to see her need of the Saviour. He had become
kinder, more considerate and attentive to her needs than ever.
She could see that true faith is not just a notion but a way of
life; her spouse lived it out day by day. Eventually she too,

though not driven by terrible sense of conviction like her husband, opened her heart to the Redeemer. She, more than any other mortal, proved to be an invaluable asset as he later engaged in Christian warfare in earnest as a preacher of the gospel of Christ.

4.

Soldier

The year 1813 was most eventful for Spencer Cone. On 10 May he was married in Philadelphia to Sally Morrell. In November of this same year he was converted to Jesus Christ after reading again the story of John Newton's conversion. On 4 February 1814 he obeyed the Lord in believers' baptism and became a member of the First Baptist Church of Baltimore.

But the editor of the *Baltimore Whig* had barely begun to experience domestic tranquility and relish a new relationship to Jesus Christ when these were interrupted by the second major war of the new republic. Trouble had been brewing between Great Britain and the American colonies for several years. American encroachment on land claimed by the British had produced clashes in the West. British ships, even operating off New York harbour, began to stop passing vessels, stripping them of seamen whom they supposed to be British subjects.

Spencer, by virtue of his position as commander of the Baltimore Union Artillery Company, was in the line of duty to enter active service, which he did without hesitation. He was a part of Major William Pinckney's battalion, and under a 'brevet commission' had taken command of one of the companies of the fifth rifle regiment. He would soon be thrust into the midst of one of the fiercest battles of the war, and witness first-hand the trauma of humiliating defeat and eventually the triumph of victory.

In August 1814 a formidable British fleet, commanded by Admiral Alexander Cochrane, appeared at the mouth of the Patuxent River, southeast of Washington D. C., obviously with the intention of invading. A collection of American militia, hastily thrown together, marched to Bladensburg, about six miles east of Washington to contest the British approach. At the time Bladensburg was a small village of about 400 people, with a few brick houses offering scant defence against the invading forces. Here, on the rising ground beyond the town, the first battle in the vicinity of the nation's capital was fought.

A British brigade of 4,500 men and three guns, commanded by Major General Robert Ross, landed on the Patuxent and began to ascend the banks, moving in the direction of Washington. The small number of American gunboats was unable to oppose the overwhelming force of the invaders, so they burned their boats and abandoned them. With a somewhat smaller force than the British, General Winder stood on the hill to contest their movements.

By a forced march Major Pinckney's battalion, to which Spencer Cone was attached, reached Bladensburg in time for the battle. By the time the soldiers reached the village, however, they were scarcely ready for an engagement. The long trek in the hot August sun, poor food and no rest had left them totally exhausted. In addition leadership of the defenders was confused due to misdirected orders from President James Madison. As a result all that stood to contest the British invasion was a group of tired, confused and disordered men. It was a disaster waiting to happen.

Pinckney's battalion was thrown forward alone to occupy a high hill far beyond the main body of Winder's army and there, unsupported and exposed, they fired their ammunition. Realizing the hopeless position they were in, the whole body deserted the field and fled in shameful panic. The efforts of the officers to rally the ranks were useless. In a manner somewhat reminiscent of the retreat of the Union army in the first battle of Manassas[1], the conduct of this battalion was evermore known as 'The Bladensburg Races'. Curiously the American army ran away, conceding their position before a single soldier was killed, as Cone's biographers recall. On the other hand the British lost 500 men who were killed and an equal proportion of wounded, and this before the American position was overrun. This defeat, one of the most depressing in the history of American warfare, took place on 24 August.

With the artillery thus routed, the rest of the American army, after a noble stand, fled also in inglorious retreat. Now no substantial opposition obstructed the victorious British, so they marched virtually unopposed into Washington. With the success of the American colonies in the revolutionary war fresh in their minds no doubt, Ross's army proceeded to reap a fearful vengeance. They burned and pillaged houses and businesses, and eventually destroyed the capital itself.

At that time Spencer's two sisters, Amelia and Kitty, were living in Washington. Kitty was married to John Norvell, a partner with him in the *Baltimore Whig* and also a soldier in the ill-fated army. With the English now in hot pursuit and pressing towards Washington, Cone and Norvell set out with great haste to seek to get them away from the approaching danger. The news had spread that the American army had been defeated, and as a result the citizens of Washington came under a sense of total terror and confusion. Soldiers and citizens of all description began to rush through the streets, trampling upon one another with no other motive than escape. Tidings of the cruelties of the British in their marauding expeditions on the southern coast left no hope for any American.

Having thrown a few clothing into a bag and taken what money they had, the two sisters prepared to leave their homes. They did not know really where to go, so they simply joined the surging masses in the streets. Their desperate flight took them past the house of the president himself and they shortly came upon a fugitive soldier who was obviously sick, weak and unable to go any further. The feather of his hat had been blown off in the fire, his uniform was torn with shot and bayonet, and his body was covered with dirt and blood. Wonder of wonders the fallen soldier was Spencer Cone, their brother.

After a tearful embrace the trio set out in search of food. Spencer told them that he had not eaten in twenty-four hours and had been marching or fighting the entire time. Soon joined by Norvell and a Mr McKenzie, who had been a part of the late skirmish, they hurried back to their house where they found some milk and cold chicken. This meagre refreshment equitably divided, they abandoned their house to the invaders and set out back in the direction of the president's house. There, upon seeing their desperate plight, one of the servants gave them a bottle of wine, which provided some much needed nourishment to the famished refugees.

They crossed the bridge over the Potomac and proceeded for three miles to an old, deserted house where they took shelter. All the furniture had been removed and, from all appearances, it was also destitute of food. After scouring the deserted mansion from top to bottom, they eventually found a barrel of flour in a dim corner of the garret. A fire was hurriedly made in the kitchen and the starving party prepared what normally would have been considered a frugal meal of wheat cakes. For them it was a life-saving banquet.

Thus relieved of their desperate hunger the whole party, overcome with fatigue, lay down on the bare floor and slept. They knew that the Red Coats would soon be upon them for the house lay directly in the thoroughfare they would pass. But no one was physically able to stand watch. Before collapsing into sweet repose Spencer told his sister, Amelia, to be the lookout for the marauding army and awaken him if they approached.

With the weary soldiers now asleep Amelia Cone slipped out and stood by the wall at the lower end of the garden where she kept watch for the rest of the night. Looking towards Washington she saw a distressing sight. Courtesy of the British army, Armageddon had come to the capital city. Flames from the burning government buildings pierced the night sky and smoke rolled like a thousand furnaces. The silence of the night was broken only by the occasional rumble of artillery and baggage-wagons and the echo of a musket shot, presumably that of some British soldier pursuing his 'work of outrage and plunder'. It was a desperate night; one they would never forget. The plantation they had occupied that night belonged to a Mr Wise.

The proximity of the homestead which afforded shelter that evening put their safety in grave jeopardy. There was no time to delay. Having found a pony the next morning, Spencer, as an officer in the US army, decided to appropriate it for the use of his family, promising the slaves present that if practicable he would return it to its owner. They quickly made a harness of ropes and attached it to a cart in which the women could be conveyed. But the animal had not been harnessed before and at first it refused to pull. After much coaxing, pushing and even whipping, however, it began to walk.

The long march from the scene of the previous day's battle had left the feet of Spencer Cone in a terrible condition. Bleeding and bruised they were practically an open sore, making it inadvisable for him to try to proceed on foot. But Kitty Norvell, who was sick and helpless, was placed in the cart, while her brother trudged along in great pain. As the pathetic procession left the area, she raised her head and pointed in admiration to her brother who had fought gallantly for his country, though, at this moment, his posture was not victorious. 'Look at the Christian soldier!' she said in admiration.

After spending another day marching in the oppressive heat of August, during which they had to take shelter from a tornado that passed through the area, the men found a house where the women could be left. It was a family of pious Methodists who, seeing the tattered uniforms of the soldiers, was most willing to take in the women. This was a godsend especially for Kitty who was nearly dead. She lay unconscious for many hours, but under their gentle care she revived.

Back in Baltimore there were two people even more precious to Spencer Cone than his sisters: his young wife and a new baby. She had heard of the disastrous battle near Washington and stood anxiously by her window every day, waiting for some word from her husband. With no means of travel other than his two legs and his bruised and bloodied feet, Spencer set out for Baltimore. Her wearisome wait was rewarded as he staggered home at last, barely alive. Having reached his destination by sheer dint of resolution, and no doubt by the special care of divine providence, Cone collapsed as he reached the door. The difficulty of this long trek can best be understood by the account of his biographer:

> When carried to the chamber and put to bed, upon drawing off his stockings the entire skin beneath came off with them. It was in this state, walking as it were with every step upon burning coals, that he had marched for two days.[2]

The young American republic had not seen a more perilous time since the darkest days of the revolutionary war. The public buildings of Washington had been blown up, the great bridge over the Potomac had been destroyed, the naval yards of the city were obliterated, not to mention the private dwellings that had been plundered. On 27 August the city of Alexandria was invested by a fleet of British sailors and a heavy levy was imposed on the city to spare it the horrible fate of the capital. The city of Baltimore seemed to be the next logical target for capture, and the invaders expected no more resistance than had met them a couple of weeks earlier. Such a calculation proved to be prematurely optimistic. In September the British fleet sailed up the Chesapeake and anchored. There it awaited orders to pounce upon its prey.

The spirit of loyalty to his flag beating strongly in his bosom, Spencer Cone soon recovered from his injuries and was ordered to Fort McHenry which guarded the Baltimore harbour. Here his rifle regiment, along with several other units who had been routed at Bladensburg, was to have an opportunity to redeem their shattered pride.

On 12 September between five and six thousand British regulars and marines under General Ross, as well as several admirals of the British navy landed at North Point and marched about four miles up the road to Baltimore. Waiting for them were the American soldiers among whom were Cone and his riflemen. Their uniforms were the same colour as the surrounding foliage, which aided their concealment. Captain Cone, who was in advance of his regiment, saw the British troops approaching from afar, splendidly dressed in their scarlet and gold uniforms. He could see from their ornamental shoulder pads, decorated with golden cords, that it was probably a reconnoitring party of general officers, with the commanding general himself leading the party. The invaders reached the knoll and peered through their glasses at the fields lying ahead. Cone ordered his men to fall back under cover. Then he gave the command to fire, and the first platoon, though at a great distance, delivered their volleys with deadly accuracy. The party of British officers was scattered, and, as it turned out, General Ross himself fell mortally wounded.

The British regrouped under Colonel Brooke and the two armies faced each other in a spirited battle. The Americans were ready now. They were rested, better trained, and had had time to muster the resolve and courage for which they have since become famous. Although vastly outnumbered, the Americans, with Pinkeye's brigade experiencing the weight of the contest, proved to be equal to the task. The battle was fierce, with charges and countercharges on each side, and much hand to hand combat. Finally the invaders were driven from the field and forced to retreat. A division of the American army under General Wilder almost cut off the fleeing British soldiers which would have meant the destruction of their army. But the darkness of the night aided them in their escape, and they re-embarked and sailed away under a cover of fire from the warships on shore.[3]

The land troops having been defeated, the British cannonade of the Fort ceased. The British armies were facing similar reversals in the Great Lakes region, and not long afterwards were to encounter the redoubtable Andrew Jackson at the famous Battle of New Orleans. Soon peace was concluded between the two countries. Spencer Cone must be numbered among the real heroes of this controversial and poorly-managed war, since he had a leading role in the defeat of the British at Baltimore. War is a terrible thing, and it is especially traumatic when two countries of such similar culture and interests are at odds with each other. All English-speaking people on both sides of the Atlantic can be grateful that ever since the second war of the early 1800s America and Great Britain have stood shoulder to shoulder against common enemies around the world.

5.

First preaching

The second war with England left the new American nation victorious, but emotionally exhausted and economically depleted. Every branch of industry and commerce had suffered from the prolonged hostilities. Hugh debts had been accumulated but there was little or no capital to meet the obligations. The owners of the *Baltimore Whig* were in the same situation as everyone else. Spencer Cone and John Norvell survived the war but came home to a business on the verge of bankruptcy. As a functioning enterprise their publication had collapsed, but their many creditors were clamouring for money. The patriotism which inspired them to enlist in the service of their country, the valour they had shown in fierce conflict, and even their battle wounds provided no relief to their financial straits.

Cone's delightful little house on Pratt street had to be given up and all contents of any value were sold at an auction. Still a large deficit remained. Sally Cone was forced to go back to Philadelphia with her infant son, leaving her husband in Baltimore to struggle on alone. The Norvells packed up and moved to Kentucky, thereby adding to his burden. Only one ray of light gilded the dark cloud over his horizon. His wife was now a confirmed Christian and they were able to share their stresses through mutual faith in a sovereign God.

But the son of Conant Cone and Joab Houghton who had borne an unnatural burden even as a teenager and weathered the ups and downs of a teaching and military profession was equal to the challenges before him. He faced his present trials with supreme confidence that the God who had delivered him from many dangers in the past would carry him through now. Shortly after his wife left him for Philadelphia, he wrote to her:

> Bear up, my beloved wife, with all a Christian's fortitude, against impending evils. Look not at the things which are behind, but have your eyes continually fixed upon the mark for the prize of our great high calling in Christ Jesus. Let not trifling cares disturb the peaceful serenity of your mind; let not even heavy burdens, however grievous to be borne, deter us from obtaining the object for which we contend. Do we suffer privation of comfort? The Son of God was content to lay in a manger for our sakes; for our sake, he submitted to be buffeted, and spit upon by sinners, and, at last, Oh! Inconceivable wonder! poured out his precious blood freely upon the cross, that he might reconcile us to God. And when this dear Savior calls us to suffer a little for him, shall we grow restive and rebel. Oh! Never![1]

Spencer Cone was a man whose faith in the Redeemer, who had saved him, clearly was increasing, and the manifold trials he had encountered had only forced him to cling more closely to his God. He was growing theologically and spiritually every day. The evangelical faith he had learned from his parents was being nourished by intense study of the Bible, encouraged by the fellowship of the saints in his church, First Baptist of Baltimore, and strengthened by his experiences in encountering the hostile winds of life. Such a depth of commitment to the gospel, resident in a man of such wonderful talents and courage, was a portent of a calling to a life of dedication to Christian service.

> The members of his church in Baltimore sensed his gifts and began to solicit his assistance in the public worship services.

Such invitations awakened profound desires and struck a chord deep within him. 'My soul pants to be engaged in the work of the ministry; but, oh! How the way is choked up!' he said. The fact is that angry creditors snarled at his heels and threatened to drag him into bankruptcy. It was tempting to go this route. But no, his honor and integrity as a man, not to mention his desire to please God, made him determine to pay the last penny. 'I cannot take the benefit of the Insolvent Act, while there is the slightest prospect of liquidating the claims against us. I am anxious to devote all my life to come to my dear Lord and Master, but were I to shake off these claims, would it wound his cause or advance it? ...I am not my own property. I cannot do what my soul longs to do. I must prevent, if possible, the breath of scandal from tainting in the slightest degree my name, or how dare I hope the Lord Jesus will make me a useful laborer in his vineyard.'[2]

An offer soon arose which appeared to provide a golden opportunity to solve his problem. He was offered a position as an officer of a merchant ship in which he would have been in charge of the commercial interests of a voyage to Europe. He wrote to his wife seeking her counsel. Should he take this job which would be financially lucrative but would remove him from his family, or should he choose 'dry land and hard knocks'? Understandably Sally vetoed this venture with the utmost of her influence. But another door opened. The Secretary of the Treasury, Charles James Dallas, through the influence of his son, George, who had been a close friend of Spencer when he lived in Philadelphia, appointed him to a job in the Treasury Department. He accepted this position, so he left with his wife and son for the nation's capital, where so recently he had endured the traumas of war.

After moving to Washington the young official and his wife joined the Baptist church there, of which Rev. Obadiah B. Brown was pastor.[3] In about a month after moving to Washington he became acquainted with a deacon of a little church which met at the Navy Yard. The church had no pastor but met for prayer every Lord's day morning. The deacon asked Spencer Cone to lead the meeting and give a talk to the little group which consisted of twenty or thirty people. He felt impressed to share some thoughts about 1 John 2:1, where the priestly ministry of Jesus Christ is set forth. This was, as he said, 'My first attempt to preach Christ crucified to my fellow men.'

He was surprised at how easy and natural sharing the gospel was. From his lips words, inspired from a heart fervently in love with his subject, flowed freely. He could hardly believe when he concluded that he had spoken for a hour. So moved were the people that they asked him to preach again the next Lord's day morning. So far as Spencer Cone conceived, this second invitation, extended in a very obscure manner by an insignificant group of people, produced a result which he could never have imagined. Somehow it became known that Spencer Cone, who had in recent memory acquitted himself so gloriously in the spotlight of the Washington theatre, was to preach in the little church on the Commons, near the Navy Yard. Could it be that the stentorian voice which had charmed and thrilled the great crowds at the stage productions was now *a preacher?*

When the speaker, who was now employed in the government office of the Treasury, arrived at the little church for his second attempt at delivering the gospel he met a shocking sight. The building was filled to capacity and a huge crowd had gathered outside anxiously waiting to listen to the actor turned evangelist. When he looked at this great throng his heart sank within him with trepidation. He was tempted to turn back and desert in the face of such an awesome challenge. But he mustered the courage and pressed his way through the crowd so massed together that he could hardly reach the pulpit. Compounding his anxiety was a voice within him that seemed to be saying that if he dared attempt to preach, his mouth would be suddenly and effectively stopped. The thought flashed through his mind that he had no right or qualification to address such a large crowd and that if he persisted his precious Saviour would be dishonoured by a shameful performance.

The suggestion seemed plausible. What business had he, who so recently had engaged in what was considered generally to be a dishonourable trade, and who even now was shackled by great debt, to stand behind the 'sacred desk'? But where did this temptation to abandon the task and slip away come from? At first he never imagined that it had come from the great deceiver, Satan, who hates gospel preaching and will spare no stratagem to hinder anyone who attempts it. He decided to postpone a decision as he went through the preliminaries of the service: a hymn, a chapter in the Bible, a prayer and another hymn. After that he would announce his intentions. As the second hymn began the issue was still in doubt. Darkness and confusion clouded his mind now bound with tension. His heart raced. Perspiration broke out on his face. Later in life he recalled that 'this was the greatest trial I ever had as a preacher, in view of an audience'.

And then, words from the old hymn lifted from the lips of the great congregation:

Be thou my strength and righteousness,
My Jesus and my all!

These reassuring lines flooded his trembling soul with irresistible force. The panic disappeared like the dank fog of an autumn morning, driven by the blazing light of the sun. It was with nerves of steel and growing confidence that Spencer Cone rose to address the crowd from Ephesians 2:10: 'For we are his workmanship, created in Christ Jesus unto good works, which God hath before ordained that we should walk in them.' Forgetting himself he launched into his theme with great energy and boldness. 'Wonderfully did the Lord help me that day,' he wrote many years later. He spoke for an hour with 'fervour and rapidity'. No, it could be better said that the Holy Spirit took over his mind and soul and spoke through him. He exalted Jesus Christ and the Spirit always honours those who honour the Son of God.

Spencer Cone went home that day with a much greater sense of triumph than he had ever had after he had electrified an audience in one of his famous dramatic roles or after he had led the successful charge against General Ross and his Red Coats on the shore at Fort McHenry.

A great victory had been won. Jesus, standing beside his new recruit, had put Satan to flight and the people had listened in wonder and appreciation as he pointed them to the straight and narrow way. He remarked, 'I felt it to be so easy to preach Jesus, and I was so ready to spend and to be spent in his service, that I consented to an appointment for the next Lord's day.' He had savoured the intoxicating power of the pulpit, and after this nothing else would satisfy. A preacher was born.

This second effort at preaching was rewarded with a third invitation, at which time he preached from Malachi 3:16: 'Then they that feared the LORD spake often one to another; and the LORD hearkened, and heard it' etc. Though he supplies no details, he reported later that one was converted through this message. God 'gave me that day a soul for my hire, to encourage my heart, and to strengthen my hands — blessed be his holy name for ever!' This blessing, added to the exhilaration of his great liberty in preaching, filled him with gratitude: 'Oh, what am I, or what my father's house, that to me this grace should be given, "to preach among the Gentiles the unsearchable riches of Christ?" ' [4]

6.

Alexandria pastorate

It was evident to all who heard him that the twenty-nine-year-old Spencer Cone, who worked in the Treasury department and preached to a little group of Christians at the Navy Yard, was a man who was destined to be greatly used of God. His evident sincerity, single-minded devotion to the gospel and remarkable skill at moving an audience soon secured for him a wonderful opportunity. In the year 1815 with meteoric suddenness, much like his rapid advance in his teaching profession, he was thrust into a position of remarkable prominence: the chaplaincy of the US Congress.

It came about like this. A widow who was a member of the little church to which he was preaching kept a boarding-house, principally frequented by members of Congress. She had two sons, aged ten and twelve, who served as pages in the House of Representatives. She was so anxious to see the gifts of her preacher more widely known that she mentioned her desire to the wife of a member of Congress, who was herself a Christian. 'Won't you ask your husband to nominate Brother Cone as chaplain to the House?' she entreated. Her guest responded by saying that she would and she did approach her husband about the matter. At her urgent request he did nominate Cone and the widow's sons, delighted at the nomination, prepared ballots with Cone's name on them, giving them out to the members, importuning every one to vote for him. Impressed no doubt by these two youngsters, as well as by Cone's preaching abilities, he was elected.

Thus the young preacher, in an intervention of providence, was placed in a position of great prominence and influence. But the man they chose was no suave diplomat or political chameleon. Of duplicity, cunning or compromise he knew nothing. In the great legislative body to which he was called to be the spiritual leader he boldly preached the gospel of Jesus Christ. A specific incident illustrates this. A distinguished congressman who had lived as an infidel became very ill and called for a minister of the gospel. Whether he turned to God or not is not known, but his alarm at the approach of death gave Spencer Cone an opportunity. After the man died the preacher was called upon to address Congress. With the demise of their late colleague fresh in their minds, Cone expounded on the dangers of delay in seeking God for salvation. With shocking frankness he reminded the audience how some live in wantonness and unbelief and then die in hopelessness and despair.

It was a bold stroke, but one that was too sharp for the tastes of some who heard him. Two sons of the deceased heard the sermon and were outraged. They felt that the character of their father, whom they regarded as a virtuous man, had been besmirched and demanded that Cone publicly apologize. Word spread around Washington that the chaplain of the House was an object of reproach for unseemly forthrightness. Some of the members of the church were alarmed that their beloved brother might be in real danger. Rumours spread that on the next Lord's day he would publicly ask forgiveness for his youthful audacity.

When the day arrived the atmosphere was electric. A great throng of people came to hear how the beleaguered preacher would deal with the criticism. When he took the platform he displayed absolutely no appearance of fear or discomposure. It was a calm and serene man who announced the hymn, and then poured out his heart in prayer. As he stood up and began to preach every eye was on him, every ear poised to hear. But to the amazement of the audience, it was no softened message that the chaplain came to proclaim. With great dignity, with a voice mellowed by compassion but yet firm and strong, he proclaimed the same rousing message the congressmen had heard. Without wavering he preached the whole plan of salvation through Jesus Christ, extending hope and comfort to all who would come and receive the proffered mercy of the Saviour, but also issuing strong words of warning to the impenitent. For those who turned to God in faith, salvation was assured, but for those who die in their sins 'stern words of doom ... went rolling and thundering through the house'. There was no backing down, no timid recanting, no apology. After all he was sent by God to prophesy concerning the truth, not to pander to sophisticated tastes.

The chaplain of the House of Representatives had never succumbed to fear, though he had faced many dangers in his young life. Counsel from his revered grandfather and father, veterans of the nation's war of independence, had welded in him a backbone of steel. At the lap of his mother he had learned how the champions of Holy Scripture had wrought victories through great courage and boldness. A gracious God had given him strength to overcome the scandal of poverty, the snares of success, and the shame of military reversal. It was not in him to shrink from the challenge of any difficulty, or to flinch in the face of any enemy, however powerful or resourceful. The fact is that a great victory for evangelical truth had been won. Notice had been served, clear and strong, that the preacher to the House of Representatives, in the warfare with Satan and his host, would know no retreat. Sin, he believed, would destroy the soul of man, and as a friend to every sinner and as a faithful representative of the gospel of his Lord, he would preach what he believed.

In the midst of this conflict in Congress, Cone received encouragement from an interesting source. While serving in this
position he became acquainted with and, in fact, quite friendly
with the Speaker of the House, Henry Clay of Kentucky. Clay,
who was thirty-eight at the time, became famous a few years
later as a result of his advocacy of 'The Missouri Compromise',
which was a measure to regulate slavery. He ran unsuccessfully
for President of the United States three times, and is considered
one of the most influential leaders in American history. After
one of Cone's messages before the House of Representatives,
several members went to Clay and requested that Spencer Cone
be prevented from preaching again. The Speaker took Cone
by the hand and warmly assured him that he should not be
disturbed in the least as he discharged his duty as the preacher
to Congress. Thomas Armitage, the historian who knew of this
incident and reported it in his address at Cone's funeral, said
that Clay 'respected him the more for faithfully preaching the
doctrines which he honestly believed were the Bible.'[1]

In every generation there are those who demand soft words
and watered down theology from the preacher. Especially dis-
tasteful to many people of refined manners and sophisticated
taste is the notion that one must be born again in order to enter
the kingdom of God. It was Cone's insistence, even in Congress, that a personal experience with Christ is necessary to
enter heaven that got him into difficulty. But he could not and
would not back down. Faithfulness to his Lord was paramount.
We can admire today, as did Henry Clay long ago, such an
unswerving commitment to conviction as Spencer Cone demonstrated. A fledgling preacher, untrained by the distinguished
theological institutions of his day, virtually untried by long
preaching experience and unsheltered by powerful friends, could
not have faced a more formidable challenge than that of preaching gospel truths to the political leaders of America. There he

stood alone before the political power brokers of his day, with the Word of God before him. But stand he did, and God blessed him. Two ladies, wives of members of Congress, were converted through the address mentioned above.

Before Spencer Cone lay a long and highly successful career as a pastor, theologian and master of assemblies. But we may well suppose that a man of such unbending loyalty to the gospel and determination to stand for what he believed, come what may, would make many enemies. Like the apostles of the New Testament, Spencer Cone proclaimed without fear or favour a gospel 'often spoken against'. His preaching aroused intense hatred at times. On several occasions his life was threatened. A gentleman who belonged to the Catholic church had the galling experience of seeing his wife come to Christ and become a Baptist under Cone's preaching. He became violently angry and went about with a firearm, vowing to put away the despised Baptist minister. But though he had many opportunities to carry out his threat, either from fear or simply God's providential protection, nothing came of it. Still the ministry Cone engaged in was one fraught with hazards, for there is an inveterate animosity of the human heart towards the gospel of God's grace.

After Cone's tenure as chaplain of Congress, which lasted about a year, he assumed the pastorate of the Baptist Church in Alexandria, Virginia. Actually he first preached in the Presbyterian church of that city, and it was this which led to his pastoral opportunity. The Presbyterian church at that time had evidently been lulled to sleep by a very orthodox but lifeless ministry. The people were in the habit of shuffling off to their spots in the pews Sunday after Sunday and then retiring in a half-somnolent state. Complacency, indifference and callousness were prevalent.

Spencer Cone preached from the text: 'Whereas I was blind, now I see' from John chapter 9. It was a searching and rousing message which emphasized the natural blindness of the human soul to the glory of God and demonstrated how God in his grace must awaken the sinner to see his own shortcomings and inability to save himself. Like barbed arrows the powerful truths of this sermon pierced the hearts of many sinners and moved through the congregation with stunning effect. They had seldom heard anything like this before.

Some women in that church determined that this Baptist preacher must find a position somewhere in their town. At that time the Baptist Church was in a very weak state, with only twenty or thirty women and one man attending. They had no pastor and no regular preaching. They went to the people in charge of the pulpit schedule and secured an invitation for Spencer Cone to speak, even promising that they would guarantee his salary if he were called to be the pastor. A pastoral call was subsequently extended to him. He prayed about the matter and agreed to come. Immediately he moved his family there, which consisted of his wife, Sally, and his infant son, Edward.

The circumstances of this first pastoral charge in 1816 were humble, but the needs were great and so Spencer Cone launched into his business with great energy and enthusiasm. He believed that as God had sent him to this city, God must have many people there. All around there was spiritual destitution. The social ills of the city, in close proximity to Washington, were rampant. They were poverty, gambling, drunkenness and infidelity, all of which are symptoms of a deeper moral problem. He had no doubt that the true gospel preached faithfully by the power of the Holy Spirit accompanying it could effect a change.

God poured out abundant blessings upon his labours. Crowds soon began to attend his ministry and the building had to be enlarged. Conversions from every class of society began to multiply. Deists were driven out of their cold and sterile refuge and the self-righteous were brought to deep humiliation over their sins. Formal professors of religion who were strangers to the new birth sought and found a vital relationship with God;

and those who were bound by moral degradation were set free
from their evil habits. The baptismal services in the Potomac
River created an excitement all around and thousands gathered
to witness the pastor planting the converts in the watery grave
to symbolize the truth that Jesus died, was buried and rose
again.

Spencer Cone's breadth of knowledge, sophisticated bearing and courteous manners drew around him a wide circle of
admiring friends. The strangeness of a successful Baptist ministry and the growth of his church enhanced his reputation and
made him the talk of the town. But the novelty of this movement eventually wore off and the theological and moral impli-
cations of his ministry eventually awakened opposition. The
infidels scoffed and the ungodly ridiculed this invasion of their
domain. He faced his foes with forgiveness, compassion and
trust in the Saviour who promised to be with those who preach
the gospel to the end of the world.

The following fascinating example of how God used him to
rescue a soul from the path of sin serves to illustrate the effectiveness of his ministry. It seems that a young attorney from
Washington was visiting two young ladies in Alexandria who
sat under the ministry of Cone. It was an evening when Cone
was lecturing, so they invited their friend to come and hear
him. He had been indulging in rather too much wine for a public
appearance, but courtesy obliged him to accept their offer. Feeling rather weary he felt that this might afford an opportunity for
him to catch a welcome nap, if he could hide in an obscure part
of the church.

He paid no attention to the hymn or the prayer which began
the meeting. But when the preacher rose to speak (from Psalm
23), his voice and manner aroused the man's interest. Captiv-
ated by Cone's personality he soon became engrossed in the
subject. By the time the message was over the lawyer was
convinced that he was a sinner before his Creator, lost and

helpless. The next morning instead of returning to Washington as he had planned, he sought out the pastor and told him his story. Cone invited the stranger into his home and took him under his wing, as it were, for spiritual counsel. Through the patient guidance of Cone the lawyer was gloriously converted and 'proved to be a trophy of divine grace'.

Shortly after coming to Alexandria he wrote to his mother: 'Duties and trials increase with years; but experience has proven that there is a friend that sticketh closer than a brother, a friend whose grace has hitherto been and, I doubt not, will ever continue to be sufficient for me. The Lord has wonderfully upheld me in the work of the ministry, and I may truly say, "He hath done for me and by me exceedingly abundantly above all that I could ask or think." About ninety souls have been added to the church in Alexandria, since my call to take charge of it, and the glorious work is still carrying on.'[2]

The proximity of Alexandria, Virginia, to the capital of the United States was proving to be an excellent place for Cone to begin his ministry. His stint as chaplain of the Congress brought him into contact with some of the most powerful leaders in the new republic. Also, Washington was the location of Columbia College, a Baptist institution which was founded to foster the newly-born missionary enterprise of Baptists. Many missionaries came and went there and visited Cone's church. One he came to know quite intimately was Ann Hazeltine Judson, wife of the Baptist pioneer missionary, Adoniram Judson. He recognized immediately her sterling worth as a Christian and a missionary and always held her in high esteem. Said his biographer, 'Words, indeed, seemed to him weak to express his appreciation of her worth as a woman, a wife, and missionary of the Cross.'[3]

7.

The spirit of mission

During the first two decades of the nineteenth century the evangelical churches of Great Britain and America were awakening to the need for missionary enterprise. William Carey had inspired the Baptists of England to 'Expect great things from God. Attempt great things for God.' His missionary labours in India had alerted Baptists all over the world to the spiritual needs of the multitudes in lands where the gospel had not been heard. The catalyst for initiating cooperative effort for foreign missions in the United States came through Adoniram Judson and Luther Rice, who had been sent to India by the Congregational Board of Missions. By studying the Bible en route to India, Judson came to the conclusion that immersion was the biblical mode of baptism. A short time later Rice came to the same position. As a result of this change both men sent their resignation to their sponsors in America who were Paedobaptists.

Understandably Judson and Rice turned to the Baptists for help in fulfilling their missionary vision, and they were not disappointed. In 1812 Baptists in Boston organized a society to raise support for these men. It was soon evident, however, that a national organization was needed to coordinate missionary enterprise. By mutual agreement Baptists all over America decided to meet in Philadelphia to create a national missionary society. The first meeting was to be held on 18 May 1814. Philadelphia was chosen because it was central in its location and also because it was there that the oldest Baptist association had been formed in 1707.

These historic developments were occurring at the time when Spencer Cone was taking on the responsibilities of a husband, parent and pastor. He was destined to have a major role in the development of Baptist denominational consciousness, and he became one of the prime agents in the cause of missions, both domestic and foreign. This was a time when a Baptist pastor in America was a virtual missionary himself, unless he was situated in a large city. As his biographers point out, 'The preacher, in the South, lives quite as much in the saddle as the study.'[1] Men such as Spencer Cone were often called upon to leave their immediate field of labour and range widely through the hills and river valleys of the frontier communities to gather the people together wherever possible and encourage them. The churches of Virginia were for the most part small, poor and widely scattered. Indeed as far as evangelical religion was concerned the whole country was one great mission field.

And so having established himself as the minister of a growing family of believers in Alexandria, Cone received many invitations to preach in other places, both in great cities and in villages throughout the country. Included in such engagements were the 'meeting of days' in which people came from miles around to meet in the open air. At such times it would not be unusual for four or five thousand people to assemble from the surrounding countryside to sing, pray and hear gospel preaching. After all, these were the days when the phenomenon known as the Second Great Awakening was at its height. Not only in New England where preachers such as Asahel Nettleton were labouring with such success, but also in the Carolinas, Virginia and even in the frontier settlements of Kentucky, thousands were turning to God in faith.

During his first year at Alexandria Cone was invited to preach the first sermon at the historic Ketocton Association. The fame of the young pastor had already spread widely in the Baptist churches and as a result all the people, the preachers especially, were anxious to hear this new star. When the day arrived only a fraction of those who had come could get into the house of worship, so a crude pulpit was erected outside beneath the trees. As the time for the service approached there was no one in the audience whose bearing and attire fitted the preconceived model. It was presumed that for some reason Spencer Cone had not arrived and so a substitute had been selected.

But at the appropriate moment, just before the service was due to begin, up to the platform stepped a youthful man, carrying a pair of saddle bags over one arm and a brown holland umbrella over the other. He was wearing a grey riding suit and a broad-brimmed white hat, not the conventional uniform for a Baptist minister. The audience was now completely still and in rapt attention as he began the service by reading the first two lines of the hymn: 'I am not ashamed to own my Lord, or to defend his cause!' The great crowd knew then that Spencer Cone had arrived. One of the members of his church who was present later reported, 'Words fail to describe the sensation created among the crowd, or the breathless silence with which the sermon was listened to by the mixed multitude congregated together on the occasion.'[2]

This rather brief description illustrates a situation common among Baptists of that day, but unfortunately rare in our own generation. At this period in history religious gatherings, such as the annual Baptist Association meetings, were to members of the churches a delightful source of social enjoyment, as well as spiritual refreshment. The meetings lasted for up to five days and concluded on the Sabbath. In Virginia huge crowds attended to hear such orators as Spencer Cone, William Fristoe and David Thomas. Owing to the great numbers in attendance, services had to be held outdoors, although the business meetings were held in the buildings of the church hosting the Association meeting.

It was a day without radios, televisions, movie theatres or computers with their access to a vast world through internet services. Then protracted meetings and Association gatherings provided a favoured occasion to meet neighbours and friends, and at a time of high spiritual excitement attracted great interest. In Virginia these were referred to as 'religious festivals'. People came from miles around and slept in homes or whatever accommodation was available. It was a formative period in Baptist history when many churches were growing in leaps and bounds, often through the addition of new converts. It was through his association with Baptist annual gatherings that Cone secured an interesting and life-changing acquaintance.

On one of his preaching tours in Virginia, Cone met and became firm friends with another prominent Baptist leader, who was later to become one of the outstanding Southern Baptist theologians of his day: John L. Dagg. This distinguished preacher and educator was born in Middleburg, Virginia in 1794. He preached at a number of Baptist churches early in his life and in 1825 became the pastor of the Fifth Baptist Church of Philadelphia. In 1833 he developed a severe problem with his throat and nearly lost his voice. So great was this problem that he was forced to resign from the pastorate. In 1844 he became the president of Mercer University where he taught theology for many years. His primary gift was literary, and his *magnum opus* was *A Manual of Theology*, which for many years was a standard textbook for Baptists of his day.

Cone and Dagg entered the Baptist ministry at about the same time, the former preaching in the District of Columbia and the latter in Loudon County. They travelled together, shared the platform, and worked side by side, while living in the same vicinity, to spread the gospel and build up the Baptist Churches. It was more than an ordinary friendship, akin to the relationship of David and Jonathan in Scripture. Of his friend Spencer Cone, Dagg said, 'We soon became acquainted with each other, and a friendship commenced which nothing ever disturbed. I loved him most sincerely, and felt honored by the confidence and affection with which he ever regarded me.'[3]

Concerning his abilities as a preacher Dagg comments, 'As a public speaker, Brother Cone possessed extraordinary endowments. Such was his command of language that in all the sermons which I ever heard him preach, he never, so far as I remember, hesitated for a word, or recalled one that had dropped from his lips. Yet his words conveyed his thoughts perspicuously and expressively. They bore no marks of previous study, and betrayed no ambition for literary reputation; but they came spontaneously to render the service which he required, and took their places in proper order. His gestures were simple, appropriate, and graceful. I have known orators who could exhibit more of the dazzling brilliance, or who could take loftier and bolder flights, or who could put in motion a deeper tide of feeling. His eloquence was more uniform and rendered his discourse throughout interesting and attractive. His voice corresponded to the style of his eloquence. He did not sometimes thunder, and at other times whisper; but he proceeded throughout his discourse with an utterance even, distinct, firm and strong, and yet with sweetly varied modulation, and with appropriate and expressive emphasis... In the pulpit he was ever solemn, ever earnest; and addressed his hearers as one who bore to them a message from God. All felt that he believed what he spoke.'[4]

Dagg and Cone shared a common conviction of the truthfulness of the great doctrines, which were prevalent in their own day, commonly called Calvinistic. The theologian and college president taught and supported these truths in his book on doctrine on the basis of the Bible. The preacher proclaimed the distinguishing distinctives of the doctrines of grace: man's total depravity; God's sovereign election of his people; effectual calling; imputed righteousness; the all-sufficient atonement of Christ, with a special reference to the elect; and the perseverance of the saints. Dagg comments:

> He was a firm believer in that system of doctrine which ascribes the salvation of men to the free grace of God. He maintained that men are by nature totally depraved and helpless; that they can be justified only by the righteousness of Christ; that they can be renewed and sanctified only by the influence of the Holy Spirit; and that salvation throughout is God's work, in which he fulfills his eternal purpose and displays his sovereign love. In presenting these truths, he never lost sight of man's obligation to obey the law of God, and to repent and believe the gospel. He preached the truth boldly; not shunning to declare the whole counsel of God.[5]

According to Dagg, who knew him as well as anyone outside his own family, Spencer Cone's religion was not one of mere intellectual conviction or abstract speculation, but one that translated into a holy walk with God. It was also a life of gracious love and fellowship with all believers, and especially brothers in the ministry:

> His walk as a Christian and his work as a pastor were in harmony with his pulpit ministrations. In everything he exhibited the man of God. He taught the road to heaven, and led the way. Brotherly love filled a large place in his heart. In his intercourse with brethren, when present, he was kind and courteous; and when absent, he scrupulously avoided speaking ill of any one. With his brethren in the ministry he cultivated the most friendly relations...[6]

It was about this time, during the first three or four decades of the nineteenth century that the anti-missions movement arose in Baptist circles. The world-wide missionary enterprise, which was inspired by the vision of men like William Carey, Adoniram

Judson and Luther Rice, was vigorously opposed by many in Baptist circles. While the predominant theology of this day was decidedly Calvinistic, and there was no reluctance to proclaim the distinguishing doctrines of grace, there were those who twisted these glorious truths; the result of which was a dangerous extreme. It was felt by some, who tended towards hyper-Calvinism, that since salvation was by the arm of God alone any attempt to evangelize the heathen was interfering with God's own agenda. A kind of fatalism had settled over many of the Baptist churches on both sides of the Atlantic.

Predictably when the missionary cause came into focus there was a vigorous reaction on the part of the extremists among the Calvinistic Baptists. Some who held this sentiment forgot that the God who purposed to save his elect has determined to use means to effect that end. The God who had chosen in Christ those whom he intended to save had also commissioned the early church to go forth and preach the gospel to every creature, and invite all who heard the gospel to come to the feast of salvation.

A growing gap in Baptist ranks developed between those who were in favour of missions and those who opposed it. The latter group not only objected to free and full invitations to the lost but were also strongly against any institutions which the church sought to use to engage in aggressive evangelism. Missionary societies, salaried ministers, Sunday schools, theological seminaries, tract societies and even protracted meetings to promote revival were vehemently denounced. In fact, in 1826 and 1827, the historic Kehukee Baptist Association met in Halifax County, North Carolina, and drew up resolutions condemning all such measures to extend and build up the kingdom of God. They not only denounced missionaries such as William Carey but also 'Fullerism', the nickname given to those who followed Andrew Fuller who refuted hyper-Calvinism in his writings and enthusiastically supported the new missionary movement. In 1832 at Black Rock, Maryland, a famous address was given and printed in the anti-missions journal, 'The Signs of the Times', which became a rallying cry for the 'Old School' Baptists, later to be known as Primitives or 'Hardshell' Baptists.[7]

Unfortunately the Baltimore Association, of which Spencer Cone's church at Alexandria was a part, had come under the influence of these anti-missions principles. But the 'old school' notion that the gospel was not to be preached to the whole world with a gracious invitation to all men to repent and believe held no attraction for Spencer Cone. He had been instructed in a still 'older school', that of Jesus Christ and the apostles. His biographers comment on this: 'In decided opposition to these principles, the benevolence of Brother Cone's heart prompted him to labor for the conversion of the world, and to favor every judicious effort to extend the kingdom of Christ.'[8]

8.

New York City

The invitations extended to Spencer Cone to preach among the churches of Virginia in various gatherings, especially annual associations, opened up for him a wide range of opportunities and acquaintances. The churches south of the Potomac, such as those in the Ketocton Association, were not frozen by the hyper-Calvinism which pervaded many of the churches in the Baltimore region, and Cone felt a strong kinship with them. They were interested in spreading the Word of God far and wide, and as a result their congregations were multiplying. The boundaries of the Ketocton Association became too wide for intimate fellowship, so it was decided that they should divide. Cone favoured this plan and when the Columbia Association was formed as a result of the division of the Ketocton, he brought his own church at Alexandria into this fellowship.

Occasionally Cone had the opportunity to preach in the larger metropolitan cities such as Philadelphia and even New York. It seemed that wherever he ministered he would always leave behind a devoted following of people who wished him to minister more permanently among them. William Staughton, pastor of the First Baptist Church of Philadelphia, earnestly entreated him to come to that great city. A congregation in Baltimore pressed him to accept a position there, as did churches in Wilmington, Delaware and Albany, New York. It seemed evident to all his friends that a wider field of influence awaited him than 'the narrow bounds of a small provincial city'. The commanding influence he was obviously destined to exert in his Baptist denomination would be immeasurably enhanced if he were to occupy a pulpit in a great city on the Eastern seaboard.

He was reluctant to leave the dear congregation where he had first learned to further the cause of his Master. It had grown from twelve or fourteen to over 300, nearly half of whom were black.[1]

Several circumstances seemed to point to a divine summons for him to look at New York City, which was rapidly becoming the cultural, industrial and commercial heart of America, as a place to cast his lot. A number of prosperous and influential Baptists, including William Colgate, had formed a plan to build a large and commodious Baptist meeting house in the heart of the city, with the express purpose of securing Spencer Cone as the pastor. Ground was secured and money pledged to make this undertaking a success, from a human perspective. Though this project did not succeed, it did turn his thoughts powerfully towards the great, growing metropolis. Strangely enough, even people of other denominations urged their Baptist brethren to bring the Alexandrian soul-winner to the city.

The international missionary work of the Baptist Triennial Convention and the Foreign Missionary Society was reaching a critical point at this time. Expenditures in the second decade of the nineteenth century were growing much faster than receipts. William Staughton, at that time corresponding secretary of the Board of Missions, recognized in Cone a kindred spirit and pressed him urgently for help. This pastor from Philadelphia wrote to Cone and urged him to get in touch with the treasurer, William Colgate of New York, and do what he could to help. 'I know the kindness of your heart,' he said, 'and your readiness to advance the best interests of the missions' cause... I write unto you, my brother, as believing that like the youth John addressed, "You are strong and the Word of God abideth in you." I affectionately beseech you accomplish all you can.'[2]

The signs seemed to be clear. The pleas of so many respected brethren, the pressing needs of the great cities, the growing challenge of international missionary work, all seemed to point to the fact that Cone needed to concentrate his efforts in a place where he could do the most good. 'Thus every interest of the Master's kingdom appeared to demand, with an imperious voice, that he should choose the most central and public point for his labors; a point from which the influences of missions, and every other form of denominational and benevolent effort might radiate to the remotest quarters of the globe.'[3]

After a visit to the city of New York, a few members of the Oliver Street Baptist Church became resolved to persuade him to leave his congregation in Alexandria. One of the attractive features of this congregation was the fact that a strong foundation had been laid there by the 'venerable' John Williams, a Welshman, who had laboured there for many years. He was born on 8 March 1767 and was converted through the ministries of the Calvinistic Methodists. After becoming a Baptist he became a close friend of the famous Christmas Evans, with whom he travelled and laboured throughout his native land. He came to America in 1795 and ministered to many Welsh immigrants, primarily in the New York area. The little Oliver Street church, which was only thirty feet square, soon filled up after he came, so a beautiful stone building had to be erected in its place. Cone's biographer described Williams' services here as 'long, acceptable, and faithful,' and he became known far and near as an 'orthodox, evangelical, and fearless preacher of the gospel'. In the 1820s the health of the godly pastor began to fail, however, and it became evident that a younger and more energetic man was needed to work with him. The congregation identified Spencer Cone as the most suitable assistant.

The urgent entreaties of the people from New York now forced him into a dilemma. He enjoyed a wonderful relationship with these people who had largely been led to Christ through his ministry. To get some advice on the matter he turned to his dear friend and respected confidant, John Dagg, who at the time was residing at Upperville, Virginia. He valued his judgement more than that of any living human being.

For the opinion of John L. Dagg — a great and good man, with the head of a scholar and a warm affectionate heart, combined with strong old-fashioned Baptist notions and doctrines — he entertained a profound and unvarying respect. In every way they were kindred spirits, and poured their hearts out to each other without reserve. We do not believe, indeed, that any two men ever entertained a truer sentiment of friendship for each other, or one more unalloyed by selfishness, than they did.[4]

In a letter in the winter of 1823 Spencer Cone wrote to him concerning the conflict going on in his mind between his obligations in his present position and the challenges of the new one so powerfully offered to him. He expresses his concern about a 'painful' separation from 'those who were dearest to him', — 'his children in the gospel'. The problem of a suitable replacement for him was a profound consideration. With an honest and objective heart he committed himself to what was most for the honour and glory of his Master. The weight of advantage when all was considered appeared to shift towards the New York opportunity.

If the situation was emotionally charged on the side of the pastor from Alexandria, owing to the tender relationship with his flock, it was also very delicate on the side of the people from New York because of a similarly strong bond of affection and respect for their own spiritual leader, John Williams. This good man had long laboured with diligence and great acceptance among the Oliver Street people. He still stood high in their

esteem, and they had no desire to harm him in any way. Indeed
the communications with Spencer Cone would never have been
initiated without his cooperation. Still the letters to the minister
on whom their hearts had been set had to be couched in such
a way as not to unsettle their pastor, John Williams. Their love
for him was not an issue in the least, the only problem was his
growing incapacity to carry the pastoral load.

Early in 1823 Cone received a letter from the church in New
York City informing him that they were, by a vote of the congregation, formally extending him a call as pastoral assistant to
John Williams for one year. A resolution of a pulpit committee
had been presented to the church with the consent of the pastor,
which had had a satisfactory decision. By a vote of 111 to 20
the resolution had been approved. It carried with it an affirmation of the 'strongest expression of love and attachment to
[their] present excellent minister' as well as 'a unanimous expression of esteem and regard for the brother' whose services
they were soliciting. The letter was dated 29 January 1823.[5]

One matter, in the mind of Spencer Cone, spoiled what
seemed otherwise to be a divinely-directed movement. He saw
a wonderful opportunity opening up before him. Clearly the
majority in New York were strongly inclined in his direction, but
after all it was only a *majority*. The difficulty was the twenty
who were opposed. Were they known? Were they set resolutely
against him or were they amenable to change? Would they
stubbornly oppose his ministry among them or were they the
type of people who could be won over by 'kindness and affection'? He was willing to come. The door seemed open. But
he strongly desired to know the character and spirit of the
opposers.

On Valentine's Day they addressed him another letter seeking honestly to deal with his concerns. As to who the opposers
were, it was not possible to know as the vote had been by
ballot. But, knowing all the members of the congregation, the

correspondents could think of none who would totally shut him out of their hearts. It appeared that the *only* reason for the negative vote was the fact that some were solicitous not to offend their aged and beloved pastor. But they assured him that the 'invariable reply' of John Williams was that 'if the church thinks it proper to call him I have no objection — I *see* no objection'.

Thus reassured the pastor from Alexandria was now settled in the conviction that he needed to break his present ties and move to New York. After mature consideration, after discussing the matter with respected Christian friends, and after fairly extended correspondence with the search committee, and, above all, after seeking as sincerely as he knew how the will of God, he concluded that he should comply with their invitation. His letter of acceptance was dated 3 March.

Having thus purposed in his heart to move to New York, he needed to explain in the most frank and fullest way possible the kind of ministry they could expect upon his arrival among them. Especially he wanted to leave no doubt as to the doctrines that he would preach. We can presume that they already knew his theological stance, for he had already visited them and shared his convictions. But these tenets needed to be reaffirmed. The man they were calling as pastor was a man who had braved British fire at Fort McHenry and courageously rebuked opposers of the gospel in Congress, even while defending his flock from the heresies and spiritual dangers of the day. He was bold, fearless, determined and confident. They needed to know it.

And so he felt a pressing need to send a final communication before taking his leave of Virginia, sharing with the leaders of his new connection what his convictions were and what the major themes of his preaching would be. This epistle, sent with the deepest feeling and unswerving determination, needed to be viewed as a contractual understanding between him and the New York congregation. It reveals the kind of theology which the leading Baptist ministers held at the time, and we might add, the kind of theology lay people in the pew were willing and eager to receive. In a letter dated 3 March, he wrote:

> In view of our anticipated relationship, it becomes me to specify the leading tenets of that ministry which I profess to have received of the Lord Jesus. It is then, brethren, my aim and prayer, through grace divine, inviolably to maintain, and faithfully and affectionately to preach, the following doctrines — viz: the unity of God; the existence of three equal persons in the Godhead; the just condemnation and total depravity of all mankind by the fall of our first parents; eternal, personal, and unconditional election; the proper and essential deity of the Lord Jesus Christ; the indispensable necessity of his atonement and its special relationship to the sins of his people; justification by the imputed righteousness of Christ alone; effectual calling by the irresistible operation of the Holy Spirit; the perseverance of the saints; believers' baptism by immersion only; the Lord's Supper, a privilege peculiar to baptized believers regularly received into the fellowship of the church; the resurrection of the body; the general judgment; the everlasting happiness of the saints, and the interminable misery of the finally impenitent; the obligation of every intelligent creature to love God supremely, to believe what God says, and to practise what God commands; and the divine inspiration of the Scriptures of the Old and New Testament, as the infallible rule of faith and practice.[6]

He concluded his letter by affirming his resolve that, with God's permission, he would be in New York to take up his new post by the month of May.

At a later stage he shared with his mother, with whom he had stayed in intimate contact, the inner conflicts he had during this period. Although he had the profoundest confidence in the theological foundations on which his faith rested and total commitment to the gospel of God's grace, he felt a kind of grief and inner sadness at the prospect of leaving his flock. The thought of this occasioned 'much agitation' in his mind. 'To bid an earthly adieu to those Christian friends whose fidelity and hearted attachment have been proved in *winter* as well as in summer, and to shake hands with those who acknowledged me father in the gospel, and leave them too, perhaps, without an under shepherd to feed them with knowledge and understanding — Alas! While contemplating that period, I think I understand the words of Paul — "What, mean you to weep and to break mine heart?" ' [7]

Beside the difficulty of severing a connection with a people to whom he was so deeply attached, he was not unaware of the difficulties facing him. While he was totally confident regarding the theological foundations of his ministry and fully committed to the gospel he loved so well, he had not the same assurance about his ability to endure the stresses of a pastorate in a large city. 'But I am depressed from a view of all the dangers, and privations, which await me in my future ministerial career.' Should he focus solely on the challenge before him he would succumb to fear. 'I am sure I should faint at the prospect, if grace had not enabled me to say, "I am willing not only to be bound, but to die also at Jerusalem for the Lord Jesus." ' He concludes, in this letter to his dear mother whose faith and prayers had helped to sustain him through so many trials, 'I look for no heaven on earth, but to preach a crucified Redeemer to poor, perishing sinners.' [8]

And so with his heart torn by these conflicting emotions he made preparations to leave the small southern city where he had first heralded the gospel and go to the great city on the Atlantic ocean which was growing in leaps and bounds, not only from natural multiplication but through the flood of immigrants from Europe. Hope prevailed over fear, trust in God pushed aside his doubts as he announced to his people his decision.

The night before he left they came to his home, two and three at a time, to bid him a sorrowful farewell. All who were not hindered by sickness clustered around their spiritual father who now was about to depart from their midst. The next morning many of them, men and women, gathered around the stage-coach which would soon provide him passage from their town. Tears flowed freely as they said goodbye. But they also assured him of their best wishes and their fervent prayers that the same success with which he was blessed in Alexandria would attend his ministry in New York.

9.

Shocks in the family circle

Henry Hudson, whose name is borne by the great river that flows into the Atlantic at Long Island Sound, is generally considered to be the discoverer of New York. In the late summer of 1609 this English navigator, in a vain quest for a passage to India for the Dutch West India Company, sailed into the harbour. As he looked inland he paused with breathless wonder as he beheld the green hills that surrounded the waterway and the seemingly limitless potential farmland in the valleys below. The commercial possibilities of this site were obvious to him, a fact that he quickly made known to his employers. This report was responsible for the Dutch settlement that set the pattern for the city's future prosperity.

Although the Dutch were the first to lay claim to New York, this supremacy ended on 8 September 1664, when a fleet sent by the Duke of York as part of the Anglo-Dutch war in Europe easily seized the city. Originally called New Amsterdam, the population in 1653 was a mere 800, but by the end of the revolutionary war 33,000 people lived in New York, now the largest city in the new nation. By the turn of the eighteenth century it had grown to 60,000.

The Erie canal, which was begun in 1817 and finished in 1825 connected New York City with Buffalo, the Great Lakes and the opening West. This inland waterway guaranteed the city's pre-eminence as a seaport and first class commercial and industrial centre. When waves of immigrants began to sweep into the area in the early 1800s vast pools of cheap labour, both skilled and unskilled, fuelled a new era of spectacular growth, although this also helped to create a mood in which social unrest could easily thrive.

The flood of immigrants, primarily from Europe, brought a rich mix of all the leading religious sects. Historically the foremost religion was the Dutch Reformed, but Roman Catholics, Jews, Episcopalians and Methodists, indeed all the major Protestant groups had a sizeable representation. The city became a see of a Roman Catholic bishop in 1808 and an archbishop in 1850.

The first Baptist minister to preach in New York City was William Wickenden of Rhode Island who laboured for about two years there in the latter part of the seventeenth century. But at that time one had to have a licence from the British government to preach, so he was regarded as a lawbreaker and thrown into prison where he languished for several months. In 1712 Valentine Wightman of Groton, Connecticut did evangelistic work in the city and baptized twelve converts. After a successful petition to the British government, this group was organized into a church in 1724, although it disbanded in 1732. This congregation held to an Arminian view of grace. The first Calvinistic Baptist church in New York was organized in 1745 under the leadership of Jeremiah Dodge.

The New York Baptist Association was formed in October of 1791. The Oliver Street Baptist Church was received into the association on 2 May 1805. Among the messengers representing it on that occasion were John Williams, the pastor and Welshman whom Spencer Cone would be called one day to assist, and the future Baptist leader, Francis Wayland. Williams baptized nearly 600 people during his ministry, which was primarily among the Welsh immigrants of New York, and by the 1820s the Oliver Street church had grown to over 500.

Spencer Cone arrived in New York City on 27 May 1823. At the time his family consisted of six: the preacher and his wife, two children, an orphan whom they had adopted in Alexandria, and a black girl, Mary, who was the nurse of their youngest child and who refused to separate from them when they left Virginia. They left behind two children buried in Virginia, Maria and William, who died in 1818 and 1821 respectively.

The new minister and his family busied themselves with getting settled in their new location. They shopped, furnished their new home, and sought to establish relationships with key leaders in the church. Their house, a short distance from the church, was half the size of the one they had left in Alexandria, but was comfortable. Their new flock spared no means possible to give them a warm welcome and to make the transition as smooth as possible. Any fatigue, turmoil or strain that attended the change of residence was overcome by the excitement and optimism of the opportunity before them. Spencer Cone was brimming with enthusiasm at the prospect of preaching in the great city.

The new minister was filled with zeal to glorify the Lord in his preaching, and his sermons demonstrated an evident love for the people who came to hear him. But he was as straightforward as he was earnest, as bold as he was compassionate, as uncompromising as he was magnanimous. The church had previously been a happy and growing one, but had limited connections beyond its own community and denominational relationship. With the coming of Spencer Cone this soon changed. The pulpit of Oliver Street soon became a major attraction to people of a variety of religious sects and social groups in New York. Just as in Alexandria, great crowds flocked to hear his plain-spoken presentation of the great truths of the gospel.

There was nothing affected, showy, or demagogic in his pulpit manners. The chief power of his messages was content, not style. His son Edward writes:

Yet he made no effort; no display. No public notice was given of the exercises except from his own pulpit. He conceded nothing to the passion or prejudices of the day. His preaching was plain, experimental, evangelical. The more the crowd of strangers flocked to hear him, the plainer he grew, divesting his style of everything like rhetorical ornament and bending all the powers of his mind to tell them in the plainest English, the story of the cross. And that was the wonderful charm. So when the young pastor, standing, for the first years of his labors, in the great city of New York, in the midst of a changing and frivolous crowd of seekers after pleasure, money, novelty, excitement — anything that promised variety and new sensations — saw them throng around his pulpit — like Paul among the Athenians, he preached the Savior of sinners.

His zeal and enthusiasm found vent in no ornate diction; in no elaborate sentences; in no nice autopsy of motive; in no magnificence of illustration, display of erudition, or trick of rhetoric; but it beamed in his eyes; it gushed and quivered in his voice; it echoed in terror the thunderings of Sinai; it hung on every tender solicitation; it formed for itself every graceful or majestic gesture; it burned and glittered along every word that dropped like the molten gold — it was true to nature, to man, to God! It was the glorious gospel of the blessed God, preached with that simplicity and singleness of heart, which is an inspiration of his Spirit, and it had free course and was glorified.[1]

His wife, Sally, who had been won to a saving knowledge of Christ through his patient witness, was a companion in every way fitted to aid him in his pastoral ministry. She faithfully stood by his side as he gave himself to his labours as a preacher and Christian leader. She was a marvellous domestic administrator, and managed his household with such efficiency that he was never distracted from his life-long calling by the nuisances and annoyances of daily life. Sally looked upon herself, not as a separate entrepreneur in her own field of ambition, but as a soul partner in ministry. His was the more public and visible position, but she had an equally important role of private support and encouragement.

Spencer and Sally loved the same God, shared the same goals, believed the same gospel, walked the same spiritual path, and fought under the same spiritual banner. Her son wrote:

> Twinned with her devotion as a wife, was her sentiment of duty. The two were never sundered. Her husband's God was her God. The faith he followed was her faith. It was his to ride forth, clad in the whole armor of God, to do battle for the truth as it is in Christ Jesus. It was hers to smooth his path, and encourage him to the strife. So she kept from him everything that might worry or distract his mind and always had a ready smile and cheery word for him... And so that dear wife, knowing him, as woman's love only can know, studied hourly how she might keep all things at home in subservience to the great business of his life, the preaching of the gospel and the advancement of the kingdom.[2]

The great king of Israel wrote that the price of a virtuous woman is above rubies (Prov. 31:9). The wonderful helpmate which God gave Spencer Cone proved this worth daily throughout his powerful ministry, and contributed unquestionably to his success. Freed as he was from domestic stress the great preacher was able to concentrate with all the breadth of his energies on the winning of people to Christ and instructing them in the faith. Her constant devotion strengthened him when the burdens of ministry were almost too great to bear. Her constant companionship, always sympathetic, ever gentle and soothing, sustained him through the rough and tumble of life. It is inconceivable that Spencer Cone could have carried on such a powerful ministry without his beloved Sally at his side. Happy is the Christian man, especially happy is the minister, who has such a wife. The impact of Sally, as well as his godly mother, upon his life is incalculable.

The grim hand of death often visited this otherwise blissful household. Spencer and Sally had seen two of their children taken from them in Virginia. Shortly after moving to New York their precious Mary's life was also cut short by death. She never adjusted to the more severe climate of New York City. A disease of the lungs, perhaps pneumonia, but more likely tuberculosis set in and laid her aside for many weeks. In spite of the constant attention of his wife and the adopted child Nancy, Mary's condition gradually worsened. The physician warned that she was not likely to survive, and this prognosis was correct. The disease proved fatal. Even more unfortunately the preacher who had provided a home for her did not have the satisfaction of knowing that she had received Christ as her Saviour. 'She appears to be entirely destitute of the knowledge of Jesus, whom to know is life eternal,' he lamented.

But an even sadder separation awaited him, one which was to occur very soon after Mary's death, sadder because of a closer connection. Throughout the trying years of his youth and the turbulent times of his early manhood, he continued a very close relationship with his mother, Alice. Probably he owed his education and spiritual development more to her than to any other human being. Wherever he went and whatever the challenges he faced, he always knew that a godly matron was somewhere on her knees pleading with God to bless and use him in his service. The truth is that the bond between Alice and Spencer Cone was as close as is possible for two human beings. She loved him with all her heart and he practically idolized her. One thinks of Augustine whose mother's pleadings and counsels finally prevailed upon him to become a Christian. Of him it was said, and the same application could be made to Spencer Cone, 'A child of so many prayers could never perish.'

Shortly after the second war with Great Britain, many of the people who lived in Hunterdon County, New Jersey pulled up stakes and moved west, some to the new settlements along the Ohio River in Kentucky. Two of Alice Cone's brothers, Aaron and Joab, were in this exodus, taking up residence near Maysville. Her mother also moved to Kentucky, eventually settling in Lexington.

In 1817 Alice travelled by stage-coach to Kentucky to visit her relatives, ending her stay in the Bluegrass region of central Kentucky. Her homeward journey, also by stage-coach, carried her through the Appalachian mountains. While running along a steep hill near Bedford Springs, about a days journey from Maysville, the carriage was upset and all the passengers rolled down the hill and crashed against a fence post. Mrs Cone, who was already in a frail condition having been an invalid for several years, was seriously injured. In addition to her body being severely wounded by the violence of the collision, she received as six-inch cut on her head, from which she bled profusely.

The nearest shelter available for her was a mere hut, used as a tavern and way station for teamsters — that is, drivers of teams of animals. It consisted of only two rooms, one a bar and the other used for every sort of purpose, including lodging for travellers. This room, which served as a kitchen, motel and dining room, was shared grudgingly by the owners. Mrs Willard, who was also travelling north to return to her home in New Haven, Connecticut, remained with Mrs Cone and provided what nursing care she could. The closest doctor was eighteen miles away.

At this time communication between the Eastern seaboard and the settlements further west was very primitive. Mail was carried by stage, and often took weeks. Her son, Spencer, was still in the Alexandria, Virginia area and it took him nearly two weeks to hear about the misfortune that had overtaken his mother. Immediately he set out in a gig, driving night and day till he reached her. With Mrs Willard holding her in her arms to soften the shocks and bumps of the rough highway, they set out for Baltimore, where the nearest relative lived. Incredibly

Spencer led the gig carrying the twosome himself on foot. The roads were at times nearly impassible, and the conductor of the pitiful party had to wade through mud nearly knee deep. They stopped along the way at whatever houses they could find to ask for brief food and shelter.

Alice Cone lived seven years after this but never recovered her health. She died on 3 June 1824, shortly after Spencer moved to New York, confessing over and over at the end of her life that she was a great sinner, depending only on the free grace of God to save her. She lived to see all six children but one come to a saving knowledge of Christ.

In less than a year after his mother's death Spencer Cone was also called upon to preside at another funeral, that of his aged associate, John Williams, the beloved pastor at Oliver Street. His text was Luke 2:29: 'Lord, now lettest thou thy servant depart in peace, according to thy word: for mine eyes have seen thy salvation.' Since the outline of this funeral message was found among his papers after his death, we know the main points of the sermon. He discussed the *character* of a servant of Christ, and the *privileges* of such a servant. The privileges all centre on 'peace with God'. The faithful gospel preacher, and John Williams was that, *has peace* with God through the atonement of Jesus, *proclaims peace* through his ministry, *promotes peace* among God's people, *enjoys peace* in his own soul, and finally *departs in peace* to be with his Redeemer.

And so the torch of faith and faithfulness officially and finally passed from the aged Welshman, whose life and ministry had touched so many, to Spencer H. Cone.

10.

Expanding horizons

Spencer Cone's move to New York City placed him in a particularly favourable situation to be a primary leader, not only in his own denomination but in the evangelical world as a whole. While Boston and Philadelphia laid claim to greater cultural relevance, and Washington was obviously the political centre of the new republic, the industrial and financial capital of America was now New York. Its broad harbours gave it, as far as advances in travel at the time permitted, rapid communication with the whole world. He knew that if the cause of the gospel of Christ was to be promoted effectively throughout the continent and the world at large, strong Christian institutions would have to be established in New York.

Cone believed that a special responsibility, as well as privilege, lay upon the Baptist churches of America to spread the gospel to the non-Christian nations of the world where 'the heathen in their blindness, bowed down to wood and stone'. He also believed that in America, with its wonderful religious liberties, the cause of free and independent churches was destined to thrive. Everything about Cone's native land was conducive to evangelistic and missionary enterprise. The seeds of religious freedom were undoubtedly sown in Europe, but in America, for the first time in history, the free church movement had an opportunity to grow into a mighty force for good.

The pastor of Oliver Street had no sectarian prejudices as far as Christian fellowship was concerned. He enjoyed wonderful relations with all evangelical believers who loved his Lord. This was especially true of the Presbyterians, with whom he had so very much in common, with their mutual commitment to the great truths taught by the Protestant Reformers and English Puritans. But it cannot be denied, as his subsequent life and practice abundantly showed, that he was by birth and conviction a Baptist. In the nations of the old world the Baptist faith had been despised, resisted and, in some cases, openly persecuted. Indeed in the early years of the American Colonies it suffered the same fate. In New England the Presbyterians and Congregationalists tried to tax the Baptists in order to support their own ministers. In Virginia Baptist ministers were thrown into prison for refusing to endorse the Episcopalian way.

But in America the principles of democracy, which were written into the constitution of the nation itself, were in every way harmonious with the Baptist faith, and indeed were conducive to its prosperity. His son Edward wrote:

It was his conviction that the system of Baptist doctrine and church government was the only pure and scriptural form of faith and practice; that from its feature of independency, the pure and simple democracy developed in its whole plan of religious association — it was peculiarly adapted to the genius of the United States of America, and needed only to go boldly forward, and to rely on God for a success far greater than it had ever yet achieved.[1]

But while Cone advocated the concept of the independence of the local churches and resisted all attempts to enforce some system of authority upon them from the outside, he did not believe the churches should be isolated. He was entirely in sympathy with the early attempts of the Baptists to form societies to educate their ministers and cooperate together to spread the gospel around the world. In the year 1817, only three years after its organization, he became a board member of the Baptist Triennial Convention, which was the first attempt to coordinate Baptist missionary work on a national scale. He held some important office in that organization until the day of his death.

He was a born leader. All the positions he had held, as a teacher, newspaper editor, and actor, had trained him to be in charge. As a commander of an artillery company, he had led the fight at Fort McHenry during the second war against the British. He demonstrated at his first church at Alexandria, Virginia that he could gather a devoted following, not only in his own congregation but among his brethren around the country. While serving as chaplain in Congress, though only a youth, he learned how to lead and inspire men.

Holding a pastoral position in a great metropolis put him in a position from which he could lead the way in many Christian enterprises of a polemic, evangelistic, educational and benevolent nature. The 'motto on his shield', as his biographer puts it, from the time he came to the great city of New York was 'the field is the world'. This text brings to mind the saying on the tomb of John Wesley, in front of the Wesley Chapel in London, across the street from the Bunhill cemetery: 'The World is My Parish.' For great men, only a great vision is fitting. Cone was a great man with a great vision.

The cause of spreading the gospel to the ends of the earth, so dear to his heart, had many obstacles. The universal prejudice of man against evangelical truths was then, as it always is, a major problem. New York City swarmed with people whose only goal was carnal pleasure or financial profit. Such difficulties preachers in all ages must face and learn to deal with.

But an even greater problem lay within the Christian community itself. Many of the Baptists who settled in America were opposed to missions. 'The spirit of missions was far from universal. A good number of churches were wholly without it. Many good Baptist preachers were so straight in the faith as to lean backward a little, and doubt even whether it was their duty to preach to sinners.'[2] Most of the Baptists around the district of Columbia and in Maryland had been infected with hyper-Calvinism. These good people, rightly jealous of the glory of God, were so sensitive about preserving the agency of God in salvation that they looked upon almost any means as an intrusion into the jurisdiction of the Holy Spirit.

And so on the shoulders of Spencer Cone, along with many other good men such as Luther Rice, William Carey, Adoniram Judson, together with pastors such as Thomas Baldwin of Boston and William Staughton of Philadelphia, fell the task of stirring up the Baptists to energetic missionary endeavours. These men enthusiastically lent their support to the Triennial Convention, the first national cooperative Baptist missionary effort. The purpose of this organization, as explained in the minutes, was 'To organize a plan for eliciting, combining, and directing the energies of the whole denomination in one sacred effort, for sending the glad-tidings of salvation to the heathen, and nations destitute of pure gospel light'. Baldwin of Boston, Staughton of Philadelphia, and Cone of New York: this was a powerful triumvirate, located in the most strategic American cities of their day. Under the leadership of the Holy Spirit, they became a united force to promote Baptist cooperation and initiative. All of these men were thoroughly orthodox and Calvinistic in their faith, but also progressive and aggressive in their approach to reaching the lost for Jesus Christ.

To the pastor at Oliver Street the Triennial Convention plan was biblical in spirit, logical in purpose and beautiful in design. He devoted his best energies to its success. Within two years of beginning his ministry in New York, by means of his preaching and private counsels, he had aroused the interest of the members of the church in reaching the world for Christ through co-ordinated efforts. On 17 October 1825 the church organized the Oliver Street Foreign Mission Society and adopted a constitution. The president was Thomas Garniss, the vice president was Leonard Bleecker, the treasurer was Joshua Gilbert and the secretary was Spencer H. Cone. This little society, begun in so modest a fashion, became a mighty force for missions in the coming years. Through the passionate preaching of their pastor and his urgent appeals not only to the Baptists of his own flock but to other pastors and churches, the missionary society raised vast amounts of money for missions, education, Bible distribution, and other benevolent and humanitarian causes.

In 1824 Cone entered the field of publishing with the intention of propagating the truth. The project was William Jones's *History of the Christian Church*, a record of what was deemed the true stream of faith running through history, with emphasis on the Albigenses and Waldenses. Jones was an English Baptist who began as a bookseller and publisher but became quite an authority on Baptist history. At that time Baptists in both the old and new worlds were conducting a search into their origins, and many were convinced that they were not really Protestants in the strictest sense of the word but could trace their history through many despised sects which were severely persecuted through the middle ages. Jones's work was very popular among Baptists and enjoyed large sales on both sides of the Atlantic. But Cone's edition, issued in two volumes for five dollars, was not a success. Cheaper versions were published shortly after his came off the press and soon dominated the market. Sales were inadequate to cover his costs, leaving the New York pastor in difficult financial straits. His only consolation was that the cause which the venture was intended to foster was significantly promoted, though others profited more personally from it. He also published a small work entitled 'The Backslider' which was more successful from a financial perspective.

In 1817 he was elected a member of the board of managers of the Baptist Trienniel Convention, an executive committee which conducted the business of the Convention in between sessions. Thus only three years after its establishment Spencer Cone became a primary actor in the development of this the first national Baptist organization, whose express purpose was to promote international missionary endeavour. In 1832 he was chosen as president of the Convention, a post he held for nine years. He presided over all the deliberations of that body, and did so with 'great dignity of tone, and harmony of design and feelings'. From 1832 till 1841, while discharging the duties of a pastor, he supervised the activities of the Triennial Convention, during these crucial and formative years when cooperative Baptist missionary endeavour was taking a firm hold in the churches.

In the midst of his many endeavours — pastoral, civic and denominational — one great motive consumed his energies; one supreme passion constrained him; occupied his mind and pressed him forward: it was the cause of missions. He stayed in constant contact with the members of the mission board, jointly planning, praying and promoting this cause dear to his heart. But more importantly he busied himself with writing to and encouraging the missionaries themselves. He knew intimately Adoniram Judson and Eugenio Kincaid, 'the missionary hero', who laboured in Burma; John Mason Peck, the evangelist to the settlers around Saint Louis; and Isaac McCoy who spent his life and energies in seeking to win the Indians of the West to the Christian faith. He raised funds for them, defended them, and backed them in every way he possibly could. The missionaries had no greater friend than Spencer H. Cone. His biographer says:

> The majority of the letters received by him from the mission-
> aries — indeed, almost all which contained any matter of gen-
> eral interest or information, he published during his lifetime,
> and circulated as widely as possible, for the purpose of fostering

everywhere the spirit of missions, by keeping up a constant
and lively interest in the several missionaries and the stations
occupied by them.[3]

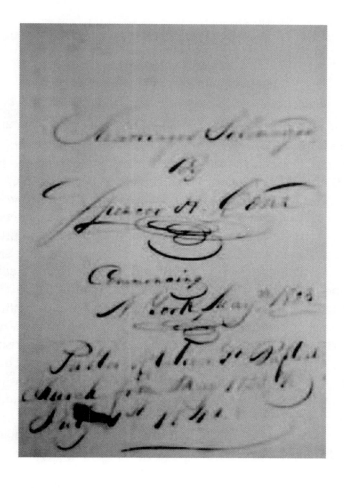

Front page of listing of marriages solemnized by Cone as pastor of
Oliver Street Baptist Church

11.

Choosing for change

By the year 1841 Spencer Cone had served as pastor of Oliver Street Baptist Church for eighteen years, and was now fifty-six years old. Under his strong hand the church had grown, as had the Triennial Convention, of which he had been president for nine years. But from 'a variety of causes' he had become unhappy in his pastoral position. Most of the members were emigrants from Wales and held to many of the customs and prejudices of the old world. They did not cordially embrace the 'strict Baptist doctrines' which were so precious to him, and neither did they share his strongly-expressed *Americanism*. The truth is that the peculiar system of government in America, with its emphasis on freedom and independence, was allowing a new attitude and spirit towards worship to take root and flourish in a way largely unknown in history. Those Baptists who had been born and had grown up in America, especially those who had felt the heat of battle in the two wars with the Mother Country, felt a peculiar affinity with the new republic. In the early years of the American Republic the Baptists were in close alliance with James Madison and Thomas Jefferson who spearheaded the movement for complete religious freedom.

There had been no serious problems at the Oliver Street Church; indeed the ties between pastor and people had been affectionate throughout these years. But change was occurring and new enterprises, carried aloft by powerful forces, were being

launched. Spencer Cone was at the forefront of these movements and he did not want progress to be impeded as he walked
in concert with them. A new opportunity had opened up to him
by a call from the First Baptist Church, which though a smaller
congregation, seemed to be more in harmony with his theology
and more open to the causes to which he was dedicated. On
21 April, he composed a letter to his flock, tendering his resignation. It began as follows:

> To the brethren and sisters composing the Oliver Street Baptist
> Church, New York. Beloved in the Lord — my heart indites
> this letter, with emotions of tenderness which a pastor only
> can feel. Many of you are my joy and crown; so stand fast in
> the Lord, my dearly beloved! That whether, as heretofore, I
> should see your faces statedly in the sanctuary, or not, I may
> at least hear of your state, and know that the gospel of the
> grace of God which I have preached to you has not been in
> vain in the Lord. After laboring among you for eighteen years,
> with such mental and physical energies as have been bestowed
> upon me by the Savior of sinners, I am constrained to resign
> my pastoral charge; and in doing this, first of all, I would render
> unfeigned and heartfelt thanks to the Father of lights, for the
> souls he has given me for my hire, and for the measure of
> success vouchsafed in building up the saints in their most holy
> faith.[1]

The letter proceeds to explain in some detail why he believed
that his period of effectiveness as the pastor of the Oliver Street
Church had come to an end. He also summarized the situation
at First Baptist Church and the reasons for which he felt drawn
there.

In a letter dated 16 August 1841, he informed his life-long
friend and confidant, J. L. Dagg, about his decision. He admits
that he had not been very happy at Oliver Street, and that he
did not feel his ministry there had been as useful as he wished.

Clearly Cone had been frustrated in his relationship with the church and he needed a change. He alludes to these negative feelings in a correspondence with Rev. J. W. Sarles, stating that his peace of mind had been so invaded as to interfere with his liberty and comfort in preaching. He determined to change his location, if possible, and about twelve months after this determination had become firm, the new opportunity arose. Obviously there are times when difficulties in a pastoral relationship are such that only a separation will solve the problem. The fact is that the problem was evidently felt more on the part of the pastor than the people, but nevertheless the time had come for Spencer Cone to leave.

Culturally, theologically, evangelistically the First Baptist Church was clearly more in harmony with the views of Cone than the Oliver Street Church. Sylvester Pier, clerk of this congregation, wrote to him on 22 March explaining the circumstances which had led to their selecting him as their new pastor. The congregation had 'long and earnestly contended for the faith delivered unto the saints' and, under the leadership of their former pastor, had 'been indoctrinated into the truth as it is in the gospel of the grace of God'. They fervently desired that they remain under the same sound teaching and they trusted that they would never be forced to 'feed on the husks of doctrine which are now held forth to our guilty race'. They were anxious that the 'words of faith and good doctrine, whereunto we have attained by sovereign grace' should ever be preached from their pulpit, with the same purity with which they had been accustomed. They were completely dependent upon the guidance of the heavenly Father in the matter of the choice of a new pastor, and had devoted specific seasons of prayer for divine direction in 'this weighty matter'.[2]

This same letter explained that a search committee of three had been selected to find and recommend a new minister, and they had totally agreed that Spencer Cone was the right choice.

The church, in the usual Baptist manner, had unanimously accepted this recommendation by a vote and was now presenting an invitation to the desired man to come and labour among them. The congregation had recently experienced 'a considerable diminution' in numbers, and they were burdened with heavy indebtedness. The First Baptist Church was a troubled but 'united band', looking to God to help them, under the direction of a wise and godly leader to lead them forth into fruitful endeavours. 'For this end,' Mr Pier writes, 'the eyes of the First Baptist Church are fixed upon you, our beloved brother, and she stands ready to welcome you with open arms to the work.' The duties of the pastor will be to preach twice every Lord's day, twice during the week, and to perform 'those other pastoral duties which the faithful oversight of the flock may require at your hands'. The salary is to be $2500 per year. It is to be understood that, except in the case of death or some 'other severe stroke of Providence intervene', the connection of the pastor with the church will dissolve with a six months notice.[3]

In his reply, dated 21 April, Cone expressed great satisfaction with the fact that the vote was unanimous, and considered this a strong indication that God was truly leading in these proceedings. He 'could not have entertained' the call, had this not been the case. He had studied carefully the basic documents of the constitution upon which the church had been founded: their 'epitome of Scripture doctrine', their church order and covenant — interestingly he had been acquainted with them for several years — and he was in hearty agreement with them. These very doctrines and policies had been the basis of his ministry at Oliver Street for eighteen years, and he had preached them faithfully, affectionately and untiringly. The other terms of the contract, such as the duties expected of him and the salary, were quite acceptable. He anticipated that the salary they offered would enable him to give occasionally to the cause of Christ's kingdom and the pastoral duties would allow some time to devote to writing and promoting the cause of missions and of Bible translation, so dear to his heart. The framework was clearly in place for a happy relationship with First Baptist, so Cone 'unreservedly and heartily' accepted their call. In mutual agreement with the church at Oliver Street, his services there would terminate at the end of June.

His goal in moving to First Baptist he sums up in one sentence. It is 'with the blessing of Almighty God upon our *united efforts*, to extend and more permanently establish, in this great and wicked city, the doctrines and ordinances of the Lord'. But in order to do this a new place of worship needed to be built, worthy of the noble enterprise which inspired him, a house which the 'circumstances of the Baptist denomination imperiously require'. They would have to give, labour and pray till this building is 'filled with spiritual worshippers'. For this worthy endeavour he forsook the place where he had spent 'the unabated vigour' of his manhood, fully anticipating that his last days would be spent in the new position. 'God grant that these last days may be my best days for your sake, and for his dear Son's sake.'[4]

It is easy to see from the attitudes and stated convictions of both pastor and people that something approaching an ideal foundation for a pastoral relationship was in place as Spencer Cone prepared to go to the First Church of the great city of New York. They loved the same God, believed the same gospel, cherished the same theological tradition and shared the same goals. The people were hungry for the Word of truth, and longed for a pastor who would give them spiritual food and lead them forth to serve the Saviour. The pastor, through many years of training and experience, was ready to teach them and care for their souls. The prospects for a harmonious relationship were excellent. It was, to all appearances, a match made in heaven.

On the first day of July 1841, after a unanimous vote by the First Baptist Church, Cone assumed his duties as pastor. At the time he arrived the church had been reduced greatly in size and influence. Various divisions, problems in relationships between pastor and people, and bad management had left them not only few in number but deeply in debt. But a success similar to that which had followed him at Alexandria and at Oliver Street soon graced his ministry at First Baptist. A core of godly people who had weathered the storms of the past had remained faithful to the Lord and supported their new pastor with fervent prayers and attendance. Many who were devoted to his former ministry followed him to his new assignment, and soon crowds of visitors began to gather. In 1850 the 'New York Chronicle' reported that this church 'has since been raised to a degree of prosperity and usefulness enjoyed by few churches even in this favored land'.[5]

One of the conditions of Cone's coming to First Baptist was that a plan be inaugurated immediately to erect a larger and more convenient building to accomodate the masses of people whom he was trusting God to send. Plans began immediately, and on 20 February 1842 the beautiful new church was opened for worship, with the pastor preaching from Psalm 20:5: 'In the name of our God we will set up our banners.' The new edifice was located at the corner of Broome and Elisabeth Streets and was built in a style known as Collegiate Gothic. It was 75 feet wide by 110 on the East side, 87 on Broome Street and 90 on Elisabeth Street. The auditorium was 75 feet square. Part of the facility, by the specific instruction and design of the pastor, was used to house the American and Foreign Bible Society, and the American Home Mission Society. The entire cost of the project, including the lot, the building, interest and legal expenses to defend the title, was approximately $75,000. The property on Gold Street had been sold for $33,000 which enabled the church to dissolve its former debts. The congregation retained a cemetery plot on Houston Street consisting of seven lots.

'It was a surprising thing,' said his biographer, 'to see such numbers of strangers always flocking to where he preached; for he indulged in no fine flights of fancy, or florid elegances of style.'[6] There is, no doubt, an allusion in this statement to the trend in the American churches for preachers to develop a style of speaking that featured a form of polished rhetoric with classical allusions, flowery phrases and flights of fervent imagination. In a day when there were no movie theatres, television sets, or the internet to amuse people, orators on the stage, platform and pulpit served as the contemporary entertainment. Such dramatic speakers as Edward Everett, who preceded Abraham Lincoln at the Gettysburg dedication, attracted huge crowds of people. It was a day when the vulgar populace not only craved to hear some new thing, but longed to hear it presented with dramatic flourish and in titillating tones. But the gospel of Jesus Christ needs no such adornment. Spencer Cone's power as a preacher came through the enabling of the Holy Spirit as God used the obvious sincerity of his Christian experience, the force of his own character and the power of the message itself. His goal was not to amuse or simply impress or inspire, but to honour the God who had called him and who changes the hearts of men. The rough edges of the gospel were not smoothed down to suit the fancies of carnal men. He spoke plainly of man's sin, the necessity of Christ's atonement and the imperative responsibility of men to repent. 'He preached to sinners, and the cross of Christ was never forgotten. He preached the whole gospel to them, with little care how much the fine skin of human vanity might be ruffled by it.'[7]

Perhaps a comment by a black sexton of the Oliver Street Church, who for so long had sought to manage the swelling crowds, best illustrates the pressures caused by the pastor's powerful preaching. He once commented on how tired he got of bringing up benches out of the lecture room to put in the aisles of the Oliver Street Church when the pews were all packed.

'I wish Brother Cone would preach in the Park,' he groaned, 'then, maybe, the people get "commodated."'

12.

First Baptist Church

The beginnings of the First Baptist Church of New York City go back to 1745 when Jeremiah Dodge, a member of the Fishkill Baptist Church, settled in the city and opened his house for worship. Benjamin Miller of New Jersey, who had been converted through the ministry of Gilbert Tennent, preached to this group of believers for a while. One of his first converts was Joseph Meeks who continued for many years as a pillar of the church, dying in 1782 at the age of seventy-three. Several members of an Arminian Baptist church in the city, having 'learned the way of the Lord more perfectly,' joined with the fellowship and linked arms with Dodge and Meeks to strengthen the Baptist cause.

The next pastor, John Pine, who like Dodge had come from the Fishkill church, preached for them till 1750. In 1747 a Baptist church was organized at Scotchplains, New Jersey and the congregation called Benjamin Miller to be its pastor. At that time there were only thirteen members in the church in New York, so they joined with the New Jersey fellowship in 1752, agreeing to share the services of Miller, who preached occasionally in New York and administered communion once in three months. Attendance began to increase under the preaching of Miller, and soon the private home was too small to accommodate the people. The congregation rented the loft of a building which was used to store equipment used in shipping, and there they worshipped for several years.

The year 1760 was significant for these Baptist believers, for in that year they managed to purchase ground on Gold Street where they erected a small house for worship. It was about this time that the church was introduced to the ministry of one of the pre-eminent leaders of the Baptist denomination in these pioneer days, Rev. John Gano. His family roots were in the Huguenot movement, which suffered greatly from Catholic persecution in the seventeenth century. His great, great grand-father, Francis Gerneaux, was living on the Island of Guernsey when the edict of Nantes was revoked on 17 October 1685. Public worship for all Protestants was prohibited and ministers were given fifteen days either to convert to Catholicism or to leave the country. One day he heard that one of his neighbours had been murdered by the Catholics and that at 10 o'clock he was doomed to suffer the same fate. With this ominous news ringing in his ears he boarded his family on a ship and sailed for America. The head of the family hid himself in a large barrel to escape from being discovered.

The Gerneaux family settled in New Rochelle, New York and made it their place of abode. Shortly after he had escaped from Guernsey the Catholic authorities confiscated his prop-erty. When he received the news of this loss of his earthly goods he replied, 'I have been expelled from my birth place, and my property has been taken from my family for only one aggres-sion, — *a love for the Bible and its teachings.* Let my name change with changing circumstances.'[1] From that time the family name was converted to the English *Gano.* This unswerving adherence to religious convictions was passed on to succeed-ing generations. Francis's son, Stephen, had a large family. One of his sons, Daniel, lived on Staten Island. He was a Presby-terian who married Sarah Britton and from this union came John Gano, the famous Baptist preacher. John's maternal grand-mother, who lived to the grand old age of ninety-six, was a devout Baptist.

John was much exercised about the subject of baptism and he determined to make a thorough study of it. Initially he inclined towards the Presbyterian interpretation and he contemplated joining that church. But the more he considered this position, the more his doubts increased. There is a tradition that suggests that he once held a long conversation with one of the Tennents on this subject (Was it Gilbert, the evangelist, or William, the pastor?) and the venerable Presbyterian took note of his anguish on the subject. His advice to the young believer is interesting. 'Dear young man,' he counselled, 'if the devil cannot destroy your soul, he will endeavour to destroy your comfort and usefulness; and therefore, do not be always doubting in this matter. If you cannot think as I do, think for yourself.' Think for himself he did, and he eventually settled firmly on the Baptist side of this issue.

Gano became a much travelled and popular preacher among the Baptists. He often took up residence in a particular church for a while, but his burden for the churches throughout the country made it hard for him to settle in one place. He began his ministry in Morristown, New Jersey, but also laboured for a while with the First Baptist Church of Philadelphia. His missionary labours carried him through all the southern colonies, especially Virginia where his preaching met with much success. Once he preached in the pulpit of a Rev. Mr Hart in Charleston, South Carolina, and when he arose to speak he was shocked at what an impressive crowd of dignitaries was present in the audience that day. Even the famous evangelist George Whitefield was there and had come to hear him. At first the fear of man seized him, but then his embarrassment departed, as the thought passed through his mind that he had none to fear but God.

For a while Gano preached alternately for the Baptist Church in Philadelphia and the First Baptist Church in New York, but in 1762 he became the pastor of the New York congregation, a post he held for almost twenty-six years. He was fiercely loyal to the American cause during the revolutionary war and became a chaplain in Washington's army. Gano was for the most part self-educated, having been thrust into the field of labour, when but a youth. He was equipped with a brilliant mind, an engaging personality, and a strong and commanding voice. He was a convinced Calvinist, but had good Christian fellowship with men of all evangelical denominations. In 1787, at the age of sixty, he moved to Kentucky, thinking that through this change he could relieve himself of financial straits and achieve greater usefulness. In 1788 he became pastor of Town Fork Church near Lexington. Although his work in Kentucky was fruitful it fell somewhat below his own expectations. He had a stroke in 1798 after falling from a horse, but managed to recover enough to continue the work of ministry for a time. He died in 1804 at the age of seventy-eight.

Many were converted to Christ and joined the First Baptist Church of New York during the pastorate of John Gano. His primary theme was Christ crucified, and many came to hear him. Within two or three years the church had grown from a small, struggling group to over 200. The meeting place was enlarged to hold the crowds, but still the building was too small. When he returned from the war he found the congregation scattered and seriously reduced. But through his faithful teaching and a gracious season of revival, the church recovered and attained its former attendance.

During Gano's ministry the congregation went through several periods of trial. On three different occasions ministers from England came into the fellowship and sought to divide it. In one instance the pastor was forced to write to England to enquire about one of the troublemakers, an investigation which yielded sufficient information effectively to curtail his influence. The church was also disturbed by a controversy regarding the use of hymn books. Traditionally they had adhered to the custom of lining the hymns, and following along.[2] The traditional

Rev. John Gano baptizing George Washington

custom of lining a hymn involved a reader who recited a line of a hymn, which was followed by the singing of this line by the congregation. But the majority apparently were inclined to initiate a new practice of discarding the tedious lining and singing directly from a hymn book. The older members took great offence at this change and fourteen of them asked for letters of dismissal and formed the Second Baptist Church of New York. One might at first be amused at this quaint controversy, but the fact is that there is still much conflict in churches about both the content and style of music which is used in worship.

Gano's successor was Benjamin Foster, who was a 1774 graduate of Yale College. While in college he was assigned the task of defending the Paedobaptist view of baptism, but his research led him to become a Baptist. Shortly after his graduation he joined the First Baptist Church of Boston, of which the venerable Samuel Stillman was the pastor. Foster became the pastor of the First Baptist Church of New York on 5 June 1785, a position he held for the rest of his life. The cause of his death was the yellow fever which he contracted while visiting a church member. Foster was a scholarly pastor, having great proficiency in Greek, Hebrew and Chaldean. One acrid controversy marred an otherwise placid ministry. Several of the members of his church accused him of preaching the 'New Divinity', a designation given to many of the second and third generation of followers of Jonathan Edwards in New England. These preachers, including men such as Joseph Bellamy, Samuel Hopkins, John Smalley and Nathaniel Emmons, refined standard Reformed theology somewhat on such matters as human ability, the nature of sin, and the atonement. In the eyes of some of the orthodox members of the First Church, Foster was preaching 'Indefinite Atonement', with unsound views on imputation. After an investigation was conducted, involving consultation with many esteemed ministers, it was concluded that the charges were not well founded and were therefore dropped.

The accusers became so bothersome, however, that thirteen of them were excluded from the church.

Following Foster, in succession the First Baptist Church was served in the pastoral office by William Collier and William Parkinson. During the latter's tenure the membership increased from 253 to 564. These years, however, saw frequent disputes over various theological, disciplinary and personal problems. In 1811 twenty-four left the church to form the Zoar Baptist Church. Charges were levelled against Parkinson which led to painful accusations and divisions. The only record of these difficulties was made by Spencer Cone himself, in a history of First Baptist which he wrote for the 'New York Chronicle', a newspaper. He seems unwilling to go into great detail about this, although the issue evidently related to how the church went about disciplining its members. 'The church,' he said, 'insisted upon *the right* of disciplining her own members.' Some of those who left the church were so irate at the methods of the church in this regard that they sent a letter to the New York Association in 1812, declaring that they were not in fellowship with the First Baptist Church 'on account of their proceedings relative to the pastor'.[3] The church minutes of 1812 reveal that the First Church had asserted in its letter to the Association that it was an independent congregation and did not wish to submit any internal problems to the jurisdiction of the larger body. The question was, nonetheless, acted on by the Association convention, with a vote of fifteen sustaining the views of the First Church and six voting against it. The feelings of four of the churches which were in the minority were so strong that they requested dismissal from the Association, which was granted.

Pastor William Parkinson, his influence no doubt weakened by such controversies, resigned from the church on 11 August 1840, after a residence there of thirty-five years. This did not really heal the breach but rather precipitated a further division, as seen by the fact that seventy or eighty people left the church upon the pastor's resignation, forming the Bethesda Baptist Church and choosing Parkinson as pastor.

These troubles left the First Baptist Church in an understandably debilitated state. Not only had some left because of pastoral problems, but many others had simply moved away. Add to this the disadvantageous location of the church building and the accumulated debt, which the sale of the property would barely liquidate and it is easy to see that the historic church, nearing its centenary, was in need of strong and wise leadership. Its theological foundations were still secure and a faithful band still clung together in hopes of better days, but prospects were not very bright as negotiations with Spencer H. Cone began in 1841. Following the resignation of their former minister the people resorted to 'frequent, fervent, and importunate prayer for the Divine guidance and blessing'. Benjamin M. Hill, corresponding Secretary of the American Baptist Home Missionary Society, preached for them during this interim period. They trusted God to send them a man of faith, conviction and strength to take the reins.

The past difficulties of the congregation, if Cone knew about them, did not seem to deter him as he made plans to move to his new charge. He was not happy at Oliver Street. The people at First Baptist he felt to be solid believers who could form the nucleus of a growing, dynamic ministry. They had borne the heat of the day and, though often forsaken by dissenting brothers and sisters, they were ready to put the past behind them and move ahead. With God's blessings, former disputes could be forgotten, wounded feelings could be healed, and they could press forward in proclaiming the gospel in the great city.

13.

Isaac McCoy

No work of the church of Jesus Christ was more important to Spencer H. Cone than the cause of missions. He once said, 'While I have my senses, the work and cause of missions must be the business of my life.' Baron Stow of Boston, a friend and associate in the ministry, gave him a high commendation as being one of the most important, perhaps the single most important patron of missionary enterprise in his denomination. 'He raised, mostly by personal effort, and paid over to the treasury, more money than any other Baptist pastor in the United States.'[1] He believed strongly in the cooperative work of the Baptist Triennial Convention and gave a lot of his time and energies to this organization which developed eventually into a national Baptist agency. Although he was not a member of the Convention when it met at Philadelphia in 1814, at the next session in 1817, he was elected as a member of the Board of managers, and till the day of his death he held some important office in the organization. In April 1826 his church, Oliver Street, hosted the Convention and in 1832 he was elected its president.

Cone used all of his talents to promote the cause of sending the gospel to the far corners of the earth. From his pulpit he inspired in his congregation a great vision to pray for the conversion of the world. With his pen he wrote articles and letters encouraging pastors and laymen alike to sacrifice to this noble enterprise. But his gifts as a preacher and writer were probably not more important than his skills as a master of assemblies in the institutions which coordinated the growing efforts of Baptists to cooperate in the work of missions. He knew how to guide a body of strong-willed Baptists through troubled waters. Stow says, 'He was always self-possessed; he was familiar with rules of order; he had a quick perception of the right and the wrong; he controlled debate within the limits of Christian courtesy; he made no mistakes; he gave no offence.'[2]

He not only worked with and knew intimately all the primary leaders in this early Baptist missionary endeavour, but also shared personal friendship with the missionaries themselves. Of all his associations with the dedicated missionaries of his day, none was more intimate and meaningful than his friendship with the missionary to the Indian people, Isaac McCoy. This energetic and resourceful man deserves to be ranked with John Eliot and David Brainerd as one mightily used by God to reach the native Americans with the gospel.

Isaac McCoy was the son of William McCoy, who was one of the pioneer Baptist preachers in the state of Kentucky. William, along with his family, which included the six-year-old Isaac, went to Ohio where he remained only a few months owing to hostilities from the Indians. He moved to Kentucky and settled near the Ohio River in Jefferson country, but eventually took up residence in Shelby country where he became a member of the Buck Creek Church. His migrations took him later to Indiana where he spent the rest of his days labouring among the Baptists of that state.

Isaac was baptized on 6 March 1801, at the Buck Creek Church when he was seventeen years of age. Two years later he married Christina Polka, daughter of Captain Polka, whose wife, as well as some of his children, had been captured by the Ottawa Indians. Early in his twenties, he followed the example of his father and became a preacher of the gospel. For eight years he travelled throughout Indiana and Illinois preaching with considerable success. Many were converted to Christ and McCoy established a number of churches in these new pioneer settlements.

McCoy's labours were in territories still contested by the Indian tribes, and his first-hand experience with their spiritual destitution awakened in him a profound desire to devote his life to leading them to Christ. In 1817 he sought and obtained from the Board of Managers of the Baptist Missionary Convention a commission to work as a missionary to the Indians. In 1821 he succeeded in getting educational measures incorporated into the treaties with the Potawatomi, Miami and Ottawa tribes. After spending some time in Western Indiana he determined to move to Fort Wayne and establish a mission there, which he named Carey after the famous apostle to India.

After many years of preaching to the Indians it was clear to him that their condition would never be permanently improved unless they were able to secure a stable entitlement to their own lands. In 1823 he devised a plan for the colonization of all Indian tribes in one general area lying west of Illinois, Missouri, and the territory of Arkansas. The Indians' right to hold title to their own lands was to be guaranteed by the American government. A territorial government was to be set up which would license traders and prohibit the sale of intoxicating beverages to the Indians, always the primary source of their degradation. His plan was that funds would be provided to instruct the Indians in all the learning of the Europeans, and also to help them to learn agricultural and industrial skills. Above all, they were to be taught the gospel of Christ by American missionaries. All officers were to be paid by the United States government and the Indians were to have a delegate to represent them during sessions of Congress.

The account of McCoy's efforts on behalf of the Indians he loved is one of heroic and self-sacrificing dedication. Like Brainerd he rode hundreds of miles through the wilderness, swam swollen streams, and often slept on open ground in his pursuit of the conversion of these uncivilized tribes. He was necessarily separated often from his family, and he had the sadness of experiencing the loss of five of his children as a result of illness.

Early in his labours in Indiana he was impeded by the anti-missionary views which were very strong in the area. Especially harmful were the teachings of Daniel Parker, the founder and protagonist of the famous 'Two-Seed-in-the-Spirit-Predestinarian' doctrine. Parker was opposed to all religious books and tracts (except his own), ministerial education and support, theological seminaries, and especially missionary work. He accused those who tried to raise money to proclaim the gospel to the heathen of desiring only to acquire money for themselves and to live in luxurious estates. Raised on the frontier of Georgia, Parker was described by John Mason Peck as 'without education, uncouth in manner, slovenly in dress, diminutive in person, unprepossessing in appearance with shriveled features and a small piercing eye'.[3] Yet with all his eccentricities Parker was a gifted orator and an efficient organizer. His efforts against evangelism and missions gained him many followers and caused Isaac McCoy no little trouble.

Not the least of the difficulties McCoy faced was the constant opposition he received from the ubiquitous Jesuit missionaries who covered the land and were tireless in their efforts to bring the Indians into the embrace of Catholicism. They followed him wherever he went, sowing seeds of doubt in the hearts of the red men and undermining his influence. Once three priests even visited his station at Fort Wayne and engaged the Indians on the subject of baptism, hoping to provoke a confrontation to the detriment of the mission. 'His conciliatory bearing,' says Edward Cone, 'and refusal to enter upon a warfare of polemics before such an audience, averted the threatened storm.'[4]

In 1830 McCoy was appointed agent of Indian affairs for
the United States government, a position he occupied until 1842.
His Herculean labours to establish an Indian nation, with all the
amenities of culture, education and self-government, though
ingenious, far-sighted and reasonable, eventually failed. He rode
horseback several times to Washington to plead on their behalf.
By 1839, largely through his constant agitation, twenty-two tribes
were settled in the Indian territory. Although his organization
plan was approved by the Senate in 1838, it failed to pass the
House of Representatives, and thus to a great extent the labours
of the noble friend of the Indians came to naught. While he was
negotiating with the government, he was continually opposed
by some of the Indian traders, the Roman Catholic Church,
some Indian chiefs, and other agents who feared that if his plan
succeeded their positions would be threatened.

Regrettably, opposition came to Isaac McCoy not only from
ungodly men, false teachers, obdurate Indians and deceitful
Jesuits but even from those in his own denomination who should
have been his friends. Although the Baptist Convention officially
appointed him as a missionary to the Indians, he got very little
real support from it and he constantly had to contend with false
accusations and slander. Edward Cone refers to 'unfounded
tales' which were levelled against him to the directors of the
mission society. In spite of 'astonishing successes' he was able
to report in leading the Indians to Christ, a majority of the board
seemed to be more favourably disposed to his enemies than to him.

It is at this point that the role of Spencer H. Cone in the life
of this missionary became significant. McCoy turned to Cone
on many occasions for counsel and prayer support, and he
found in the New York pastor a true friend and helper. McCoy
often visited the Cone household and all the family knew him
intimately, including the children. They believed strongly in his
integrity, soundness in the faith and had numerous opportunities

to observe first-hand how faithful he was to the cause of his Lord. Cone's support and advocacy of McCoy's missionary work was steady, constant and effectual. On more than one occasion he pleaded his case before the Baptist Missionary Society and stood forthright against all his accusers. Heman Lincoln, an influential Baptist pastor and teacher at the Newton Theological Institute, identified him as the best friend McCoy ever had: 'Our friend, Isaac McCoy, who devoted his life to the benefit of the red men of the forest, depended more upon his counsel and assistance than upon any other individual.'[5]

In 1830 McCoy stayed for several weeks with the Cone family in New York in circumstances which illustrate both the sterling character of the missionary and the tender relationship he had with the pastor of the First Baptist Church. At the time the state of Indian affairs was being debated in the United States Congress and was much on the minds of all Americans. Such matters as the removal of the various tribes from their native territories in the east and the establishment of permanent settlements in the west were being discussed. Unfortunately, many political leaders had no sympathy for the plight of the Indians, much less any Christian vision for their spiritual improvement. McCoy travelled to Philadelphia to meet with leaders to plead the cause of the Indians. He wanted to be sure that those who led the nation and the church had a knowledge of all the facts as their deliberations proceeded.

On 13 February he left Philadelphia for New York to see his 'untiring friend', as he called him. Only a few miles outside the city the stage coach capsized, and with its 'vast weight' fell upon the missionary who was pinned underneath. From the pain in his shoulders and chest he knew that he had suffered a serious injury of some sort, but he managed to make it to New York. Cone's biographer, his son Edward, recalled well the circumstances of McCoy's arrival:

It was a cold winter day and when he came to the door the servant admitted him. He put off his overcoat and asked for water to wash his face and hands. He then sat down in the parlor and quietly awaited the return of some of the family. Thus he sat for more than an hour. When the pastor and his wife came in, after exchanging the usual greetings of friends who had not seen each other in a long time, he said quietly, 'We have had an accident coming from Philadelphia, and I fear I am seriously injured. I believe, Brother Cone, some of my ribs are broken.' As it turned out not only were ribs broken but his shoulders were serious injured as well. This accident left Isaac physically disfigured the rest of his life.

For the next six weeks the parsonage of Spencer Cone became the hospital for his friend. For many days he was barely able to move. But in the tender and compassionate care of this Christian family, the missionary finally recovered and was able to go about his work. The pastor himself, both from necessity and from choice, was his constant nurse. Since he was unable to move himself even in bed, his host gently moved and handled him as he would a child. 'Nothing could be more touching,' said Edward, 'than to see those two men, whose lives were governed by the same lofty sentiment of devotion to the cause of human regeneration, giving and receiving from each other the tenderest evidences of an almost womanly affection.'[6]

The Cone family had an opportunity during these days of convalescence to get to know intimately the character of the guest in their home; and it made a permanent impression on them. In his own quaint way, Edward Cone gave witness to the Christ-like person who stayed in their home in the winter of 1830:

Isaac McCoy was one of the most lovable men we ever had the happiness of being acquainted with. Living his whole life amongst wild Indian tribes, and wilder frontiers-men; living a life of exposure, vicissitude, and hardships scarcely to be described; always in the saddle or the camp, and every day risking life and limb to preach the gospel amongst those whom all the rest of the world seemed to conspire to destroy or forget — his mind and manners, instead of becoming rude or hard in these rough uses and associations, grew, all the while, softer, holier, and more loving. Nothing could be finer than his manners. Never familiar, and carrying in his quiet eye an indescribable something, which prevented any one from ever being familiar with him, he never repelled. On the contrary, he attracted; children loved him. Men were compelled to feel, in his company, that they were near something good, kind and noble. The warm coloring of the heart tinged his words and manner, quiet as they were, in everything he did or said. If you had done anything true or good, you knew he loved you for it. When he looked at you, you felt that there was no selfish thought or scheme working in his mind; but that he was thinking what he could do for your benefit, or happiness, or for the benefit of some poor soul that was in need of other's help and kindness.[7]

The financial support he received from the churches was so meagre that McCoy had to sustain his family through various jobs he took with the federal government, often through the recommendation and influence of Spencer Cone. In addition to having minor positions in and about the Indian reservations, he was for a while a surveyor of government lands. Had he wished, his position as a surveyor could have made him a rich man. In many instances he was the agent to manage the cessation of the Indian lands to the United States government. Whenever such transactions took place, the Indians insisted that one of the conditions of the exchange was that Isaac McCoy would receive a part of the land conveyed, and there is no question that the federal officials, with the Indians encouragement, would not have objected to this arrangement. But the missionary was not interested in their lands but in them. In order to avoid any appearance of selfish interest, he refused to accept any property which was being transferred from the Indian tribes to the government. In order to preserve the integrity of his witness he chose a life of sacrifice and privation rather than 'ease and opulence'.

The Scriptures set before us many examples of unselfishness and devotion to noble ideals which modern Christians can follow. Supreme, of course, is the life of our Lord and Saviour Jesus Christ who came not to be ministered to but to minister and give his life a ransom for many. Elijah, who stood against the prevailing idolatry in the days of the wicked Ahab, demonstrated courage and boldness in difficult times. Jeremiah, who was called to warn his nation faithfully of coming judgement, with a broken heart and weeping eyes, is a worthy example of compassion for uncaring people. Saul of Tarsus, a rising star in his nation, brilliant, confident, and destined no doubt to be enshrined as one of the greatest Jewish scholars of all time, gave it all up to be a martyr for the cause of Jesus Christ. But in our Christian history we also have credible records of many whose lights shone faithfully for Jesus Christ, shining all the more brightly because they burned in the midst of pain, privation and suffering. Such was the Indian agent and friend Isaac McCoy, whose life of selfless consecration to his Master, has, unfortunately, lain hidden in the dusty binds of Baptist archives. Of such 'the world was not worthy'.

14.

The great division

When, on 12 April 1861, the Confederate guns on the banks of the harbour at Charleston opened fire on Fort Sumpter there was no damage to human life. The shells knocked out huge chunks of the fort's southeast corner, destroyed the officers' quarters and shot down the flag staff, but not a single man was killed. However, the damage to the national and political life of the United States was colossal, so much so that it took a mighty four-year military struggle to bring about the unity of the nation once again. The truth is that the breaking out of hostilities that inaugurated the Civil War, was the final result of a serious ideological, regional and social cleavage that had been developing for years.

The question of slavery had been debated for many decades not only in the halls of Congress but also in Baptist churches and associations. Shortly after the Revolutionary War many Baptists began to question the validity of slavery as a practice among Christians. In 1787 the Ketockton Association determined 'that hereditary slavery was a breach of the divine law', and a committee was appointed to suggest a plan for its eradication. But this debate so agitated the churches that the association deemed it the part of wisdom to drop the matter. John Leland presented a resolution to the Virginia Baptist General Committee in 1789 which called upon the Legislative Assembly of the state to abolish slavery gradually and to free slaves in a manner consistent with good policy. The next year that association claimed neutrality on that issue and resolved that the matter would be left to the individual conscience.

Baptists all across America had professed a deep concern for the spiritual welfare of Negroes and imposed upon their slave-holding members a strict code to regulate the religious care and treatment of the slaves. In many communities they were given a section in the meeting-houses for worship, but they were not permitted to vote in the business meetings. In this regard, however, the churches were only following the short-sighted and discriminatory policies of the nation itself, for even in the North Negroes were considered citizens but were without voting privileges.

As the question of the owning of slaves began to arouse public feeling in the churches, three distinct positions emerged. First, there were the abolitionists, primarily in the North, who argued that the whole institution of slavery was inhumane and immoral. Second, there were those in the South, where the whole economy depended to a great extent upon the use of Negroes to work in the cotton fields, who defended this practice, even appealing to certain texts in the Bible. Third, there was a large group in the middle, which probably encompassed the majority, who felt that the whole issue was a civil matter and should not be an issue in the churches. Many leaders felt that unity in education, missions and benevolence was too important to sacrifice on the altar of the debate on slavery.

Almost from its beginning in 1814 the Baptist Triennial Convention was in a fierce debate on the question of the correct Christian position towards slavery and race relations. Like his friend Henry Clay, the Kentucky statesman, who devoted practically a lifetime to promote a compromise, Spencer Cone was one of those who took a mediating position. As forthright and determined as Cone was on some matters, in this debate he clearly aligned himself with the broad middle group who wanted to avoid division.

As the chairman of the board of the Baptist Missionary Society, he exerted all his parliamentary and diplomatic skills in seeking to prevent an open rupture between the Baptists of the North and those of the slave-holding South from occurring. In fact, when the Convention met in Baltimore in 1841, he managed almost single-handedly the discussions and deliberations so that they did not result in open schism. But there were forces at work so powerful that even a man of the stature of Spencer Cone could not repel them. Like a gathering hurricane in the southern Atlantic, a mighty struggle was being set in motion which would not only tear apart the new republic of America but also cause painful separations between all the evangelical denominations, with the single exception of the Episcopalian community.

In 1840 an anti-slavery movement met in New York City to convince Baptists, who heretofore had cooperated in missions whatever their views, to go on record as condemning slavery. This was an early attempt to organize and propagandize radical feelings against this institution which had been fomenting in the North. Included in this group were some Baptist missionaries in Burma who had severed their connection with the Triennial Convention and had formed a rival organization which had a stated policy of non fellowship with slave-holders.

Baptists of the South with slaves, sensing the direction in which things were moving, adopted a resolution to withhold funds from the Board of Foreign Missions, as well as from the American and Foreign Bible Society, until they were assured that these agencies had no connection with the abolitionist movement. They also resolved that if a satisfactory answer were not given they would form a southern board through which they could transmit their missionary offerings. In response to this initiative the Board of Managers of the Convention made a statement on 2 November affirming that they had no right to do or say anything with respect to slavery. Unquestionably the influence of Spencer Cone can be seen in this neutral posture. The fears of the Alabama Convention, which had taken a lead in these negotiations, were allayed for a time; but abolitionist sentiment was growing powerfully and a heated argument could not be avoided for ever.

At the Baltimore Trienniel Convention in 1841 the subject of slavery was on everyone's mind and the air was electric. The delegates at the two extremes were ready for a fight to the finish, and the middle group headed by Spencer Cone was making a final effort to bring calm to a troubled situation. In a secret caucus of northern moderates and southerners a compromise article was submitted, 'discouraging innovation and "new tests" and disclaiming participation in the doings of the abolition Baptists'. The position these men took was that 'slavery was a subject with which the Convention had no right to interfere'. The same viewpoint was affirmed by the Baptist Home Missionary society.

But the 'Baltimore Compromise' was not agreeable to many of the northern men who were in no mood to settle the dispute on a neutral basis. When fierce objections were raised against the compromise the board members insisted that they were not personally defending slavery, but simply seeking to strengthen the delicate cord of Baptist fellowship. But the anti-slavery movement was growing in leaps and bounds throughout the North and what many considered a political and civil dispute was rapidly becoming a religious and moral issue. The militant advocates of personal freedom in the Baptist denomination, like those in the larger political arena, were clearly determined that their views would prevail.

By 1844 the disagreement over slavery in the Baptist denomination could be likened to a giant continental wide fault, which needed only a mild earth tremor to cause a final split. At the time there were about 700,000 Baptists in the country, many of whom were supportive of the Triennial Convention which was celebrating its thirtieth anniversary. The Convention was being held at Philadelphia and there were 406 delegates, disproportionately represented by the North. Massachusetts, the most abolitionist of all the American states, sent 103 representatives for its 31,843 Baptists. Pennsylvania had 46 delegates for its 28,044 constituent Baptist members. But Virginia, with 82,732 Baptists, had only 43 delegates present. All in all there were only 80 from below the Mason Dixon Line. Distance was part of the cause of this disparity, no doubt.

Although Southerners had always been a minority in the Convention, it had been led by someone from the South for twenty-one out of its thirty years. W. B. Johnson, a Southerner, announced his retirement from the presidency for health reasons. Dr Francis Wayland of Rhode Island, a moderate on the abolition question, was selected to succeed him and J. B. Taylor of Virginia became secretary. Sharp disagreement on the slavery issue broke out at the very beginning of the Convention. Dr Richard Fuller, a pastor from South Carolina and a slave-owner, presented a resolution that the Convention restrict itself solely to the matter of missions. Spencer Cone agreed that the issue of slavery should not be on the agenda of the Convention, and he supported this resolution. But Dr Nathaniel Colver, pastor of Tremont Temple, Boston, argued strongly from the platform that the matter of slavery could not be avoided.

The sponsors of the original resolution, seeing the controversy it was causing, withdrew it. Dr George B. Ide, pastor of the First Baptist Church in Philadelphia, then proposed in a similar, but slightly altered resolution, that the Convention adopt a non-committal policy on the institution of slavery, siding with moderates like Cone. He urged the members to continue to cooperate in the work of foreign missions, repudiating 'all sanction either expressed or implied, whether of slavery or of anti-slavery,' though individuals could have the freedom to express their own convictions on the matter. This resolution was passed unanimously without discussion. 'The Home Mission Society again declared its neutrality by a vote of 123 to 61, but appointed a committee to consider amicable dissolution of the Society.'[1]

To Baptists of the South the official neutrality of the Convention seemed merely to paper over the cracks in the wall of Baptist cooperation. The action of the Home Mission Society indicated that they would be eventually disenfranchised. It appeared to them that the only way to determine whether they were welcome as equal participants in mission enterprise would be to present a test case to the Convention. A few days after the Triennial Convention had adjourned, they instructed the executive committee to recommend to the Board of the Home Mission Society James E. Reeves of Georgia for appointment as a missionary to the Cherokee Indians. They informed the committee that Mr Reeves was a slave-holder and candidly stated that this was to be considered a test case of whether a slave-holder could be approved. After five marathon meetings and much debate, in October the committee announced that by a seven to five vote Reeves was to be rejected as a missionary applicant. The die was now cast.

Following this the Alabama Convention, in correspondence with the Board of Foreign Mission, requested a guarantee that slave-owners would have equal privileges with non slave-owners in appointment to foreign missionary service. In December the Board sent back an answer, which was in reality a departure from the position which the Convention had taken at its annual meeting. The decision was: 'If any one should offer himself as a missionary, having slaves, and should insist on retaining them as property, we could not appoint him. One thing is certain, we can never be a party to any arrangement which would imply approbation of slavery.'[2] Clearly men with an abolitionist mindset were gaining control of the machinery of the missionary societies.

Following the decision of the Board of Foreign Mission, fierce debate began to rage all across the churches of the denomination. Leaders from the North and the South laboured mightily to quench the fires of controversy, but in the end the tension was simply too great to overcome. In April 1845 the American Baptist Home Mission Society decided that it would be better if the North and the South had separate missionary organizations. Immediately Baptists of Virginia, the largest and most influential of all the Southern brethren, issued a call for a convention to be held in May. 328 delegates from churches of the South met at Augusta, Georgia, to organize the Southern Baptist Convention. From the very start the Southern Baptist Convention was a more centralized type of organization than its northern counterpart. In the North mission work had been carried on by more or less independent societies, but the Southern Baptists organized a central committee which was given executive control over all aspects of denominational life, including missions.

Spencer Cone did not agree with the decision of the Home Mission Society to exclude slave-holders and he expressed his views openly. Concerning this he wrote, 'I regret this result, and did all in my power to prevent it, believing as I do, that the constitution knows nothing of slavery or anti-slavery. I besought the brethren to act as we always had done, until, the constitution should be altered.'[3] With the New York pastor the whole issue was to be regarded as one on which sincere Christians could disagree. In his view the primary consideration ought to have been to maintain the status quo of the missionary enterprise and to preserve Baptist unity. Whether his philosophical sentiments were with the northern men who argued against slavery from the standpoint of human dignity or with the southern men who felt that the inherent evils of this practice should be changed gradually, he never expressed himself. But he did live long enough to realize that the controversy, in practice, could admit of no middle ground. Ultimately the controversy would be settled (ten years after his death) not in debates in Congress or in religious conventicles but on a thousand bloody battle fields, stretching from Wilson Creek to Manassas and from Gettysburg to New Orleans.

After he saw that it was impossible for the two Baptists groups to work in harmony in the same convention, Cone did all he could to bring about an amicable and peaceful separation. He even advocated that the money which the Southerners had invested in the treasury of the Convention be repaid 'to the last cent'. The truth is that the division of northern and southern Baptists was managed with great courtesy and good will, considering the intense feelings on both sides. Men like Spencer Cone and Francis Wayland in the North and J. L. Dagg and W. B. Johnson in the South loved one another and deeply regretted the division. They parted friends, knowing that their allies and supporters might meet some day on fields not with arguments but with rifles and cannons. After over 150 years, needless to say, history has vindicated the moral superiority of the abolitionist position, and, in fact, the Southern Baptist Convention has condemned not only the abominable institution of slavery but has also, by firm resolution, repudiated and apologized for latent racism which has too often lurked in its ranks.

15.

The Bible translation controversy

The subject of this biography, as can be seen from previous material, is a man whose life demonstrated a remarkable balance of talent, interest and initiative. As a preacher, pastor, missions advocate and parliamentarian he had few peers. Seldom has such courage, zeal, theological perception, magnanimity, and childlike devotion to the Redeemer joined in one personality. Friend and foe alike recognized that he was one of the great men of his generation. The Baptist historian, Thomas Armitage, said of him that he was 'by nature, a man of mark, and would have been a leader in any sphere of life'.[1]

The great subjects of his pulpit ministry were, by common acknowledgement, the primary themes that concern the needs of fallen man and his redemption through the grace of God. He was not given to majoring on minors or expending his time and energies on issues which divided the godly line of Christian warriors who travelled in the mainstream of evangelical thought.

This having been said, it is evident, however, that Cone's life and ministry cannot be understood or explained except in the light of the fact that he was a convinced Baptist. He knew enough about the history of the church to realize that Baptists had been, from time immemorial, in the forefront of the battle for freedom of conscience for all peoples in all lands. From his grandparents and parents he learned the importance of the principle of religious liberty, and the awful cost many of his forebears had paid to secure it. The cherished conviction of Baptists that worship is to be voluntary, completely beyond the power of any civil institution to interfere, was one for which he was willing to fight, and, if need be, sacrifice all.

In the address which he delivered at the close of the first anniversary of the American and Foreign Bible Society he alluded to the importance he attached to the *voluntary principle*, for which Baptists had so long contended. 'The Baptists in every age and in every clime, from the days of Paul, when the sect was everywhere spoken against, to the present hour, have been the steadfast friends of the *voluntary principle*, in whatever pertains to religion. They maintain, to use the language of a forcible writer, "that man cannot be born into a system of faith, nor be surrendered in infancy or age to a form of religion, but may assert his right to judge for himself; examine and decide, under the lofty conviction that God has not made him a slave." ' [2] Like all Baptists he believed that religious affiliation should not come about through an involuntary rite or compulsion of any kind but of *choice*.

Cone lived in the day when the memories of the suffering of Baptists and other non-conformists to state-sponsored religions were fresh in people's minds. The hated 'compulsory system', the notion that the state or an all-powerful church can lord it over the conscience, still cast a dark cloud over the minds of the descendants of an earlier generation of Baptists. In Europe the history of the Anabaptists was written in blood. In the valleys of the Piedmont, in Germany, Bohemia, France and Wales they were hounded from their homes and churches and found refuge only in remote mountains or in exile from their native lands. Even in America some, with whom they had much in common, found no quarter for the despised immersionists. In New England they were forced to pay taxes to support the Presbyterians and fined and jailed for stubborn refusal to abandon their principles. The same was true in Virginia, where the Anglican Church dominated the government before the days of American independence.

Edward Cone cites a book written by Professor Thomas Curtis, widely read among Baptists in the ninetheenth century, which expressed sentiments endorsed by his father and many other Baptist leaders. This volume, *The Progress of Baptist Principles*, lists five 'distinctive principles of Baptists':

1. Freedom of conscience, and the entire separation of Church and State;
2. A converted church membership;
3. Sacraments inoperative without choice and faith;
4. Believers, the only scriptural subjects of baptism;
5. Immersion always the baptism of the New Testament.

Cone would have repudiated the very word 'sacraments,' for this designation conveys some saving efficacy in the rites of baptism and the Lord's Supper. For him, as would have been the case for Baptists generally, these were simply 'ordinances of the gospel'. Otherwise, the list coincided with his own outlook.

Even a cursory glance at these Baptist 'distinctives' will show that Paedobaptists, while agreeing with their Baptist brethren on many of the main points of historic Christianity, would have been at odds with them on the last of these four points. Most American Christians today would affirm a belief in freedom of conscience and separation of Church and State, though in the early days of the republic Baptists stood almost alone on this principle.[3] But Baptists and other groups emerging from the mainline denominations still hold differing views on the basis of church membership and the mode and the subjects of baptism.

In the mind of Spencer Cone there was a close connection between religious freedom, or opposition to 'the compulsory system', and the notion of believer's baptism. He regarded the practice of incorporating baptized infants, who obviously cannot know the meaning of the ceremony, into the visible church as related to some degree to the idea that the state can 'force' a particular spiritual connection upon someone against his will. From our vantage point today, no doubt, we see things somewhat differently from the way he did. Baptist views on freedom of conscience in religious matters have gained the upper hand in the United States, and are written in the first amendment. Even Roman Catholics, by profession at least, have been to this extent 'protestantized' in America. But the patrons of religious liberty in the early decades of the ninetheenth century did not look, by any means, upon this battle as won. They were strongly opposed to any attempt to enforce a certain form of worship, either by the sword of secular power or by the administration of religious rites to unconscious infants.

Cone's strong convictions on spiritual freedom and voluntary religion help to explain the depth of his involvement in the last great conflict of his life, one that contributed immensely to the burden of his old age and perhaps even hastened his exit from this world of sorrows. He was the primary leader in an attempt to promote 'pure translations' of the Bible, not only in foreign lands where missionaries were just beginning to bring the message of salvation to the heathen, but also to people in the English-speaking world. A brief explanation of this painful, protracted debate which disturbed not only the Baptist churches of America but also other Protestant denominations is now in order.

In 1809 a young Englishman, William Colgate, came week after week to worship at the First Baptist Church of New York City, and kept in his pew a Bible which had been given to him by his father. This book, cherished for many reasons, was unfortunately stolen, much to its owners chagrin. But good came out of this theft, for Colgate realized that Bibles must be scarce for someone to go to such lengths to get one, so he set about to form a society to provide Bibles for the public. This was one of the first efforts to provide Bibles in abundance to the growing peoples of the new nation.

Similar efforts to publish and propagate the Bible started to spring up in various places. But a major coordinated effort began on 11 May 1816 when thirty-five local societies in different parts of the country sent delegates to New York for the purpose of organizing a Bible society which would coordinate the efforts of all the smaller groups. Baptists were among the most enthusiastic and generous supporters. In 1830 the new organization, known as the American Bible Society, appropriated $1,200 for the printing of Adoniram Judson's 'Burman Bible' through the Baptist Trienniel Convention. There were no strings attached to this project and it was well known that the family of words which referred to baptism, when translated into the Burman language, would connote immersion. By 1835 the society had given $18,000 for the same purpose.

In 1835 Samuel Pearce, the Englishman who worked so close with Andrew Fuller and William Carey in the cause of missions, asked the society to aid in the printing of the Bengali New Testament, which was to be translated on the same principle as Judson's Bible. A committee of seven met to consider the application, and issued a report contending that they had liberty to support only translations which conformed to the principle followed in English translations. What this meant was that the Greek words referring to baptism were to be 'transferred', or as we would say transliterated, and not translated at all. In other words, the meaning of the original Greek word, which means to 'dip' or 'immerse' was not to be conveyed in the foreign languages. The society did, however, appropriate $5,000 to be used by the Baptists, provided that they did not convey the idea of immersion in their translations.

The Baptists on the foreign fields who were seeking to translate and distribute the Bible to the ignorant pagans had, of

course, been guided by the reasonable and scholarly principle
that they were to convey the exact and original meaning of the
Greek and Hebrew texts, as far as they understood them. This
meant that, true to their own principles, they could not but render
the word 'baptizo' as immerse. The decision of the committee
of the Bible society created an immediate crisis and forced the
Baptists to convene and take a decision on what to do. The
problem was serious. Up to that time the Baptists had contributed at least $170,000 to the treasury of the Bible society, which
included a large legacy from John F. Marsh.

Many Baptists were at the meeting of the American Bible
Society on the twelfth of May when the restrictive policy was
adopted and implemented. In reaction to this action 130 of
them convened for deliberation on the thirteenth in the Oliver
Street Baptist Church, where Spencer Cone was the pastor, with
Nathaniel Kendrick in the chair. These men considered it necessary to form a new Bible society at once, and on that day the
American and Foreign Bible Society was formed, subject to the
decision of the Trienniel Convention which was to be held in
Philadelphia. This society was formed 'to promote a wider circulation of the Holy Scriptures, in the most faithful versions that
can be procured'. In three months $13,000 had been raised for
the translation and circulation of the Bible in Asian languages.

The first general convention of the American and Foreign
Bible Society was held on 26 April 1837 with 390 members
present from churches, associations, state conventions, education societies and other bodies, representing 23 states and
the District of Columbia. Rufus Babcock of Pennsylvania was
elected to be the new president and Abiel Sherwood of Georgia and Baron Stow of Massachusetts as secretaries. The Baptist leaders, who were present and cooperating in this venture,
included such outstanding leaders as Heman Lincoln from
Massachusetts, Francis Wayland from Rhode Island, William
Colgate and Spencer Cone from New York, William Brantly

and A. D. Gillette from Pennsylvania, and J. B. Taylor and J. B. Jeter from Virginia.

Although these notables were vitally interested in translating the Bible, they held different opinions with respect to the particular course to be taken. Some felt that they should continue to cooperate with the American Bible Society; others thought that their particular views on baptism were to be incorporated only into foreign translations; while still others believed that a new translation more faithful to the Greek language should be issued in English as well. They engaged in a heated debate for three days, and although some 'undesirable' remarks were made, for the most part an excellent spirit prevailed.[4] Among the resolutions adopted was the policy that 'the society confine its efforts during the ensuing year to the circulation of the Word of God in foreign tongues'. That particular point was destined to become a source of immense trouble later. When a permanent constitution was adopted, Spencer Cone was chosen as president and William Colgate was elected treasurer.

The American and Foreign Bible Society carried out its mission admirably for many years and Baptists across the country continued to contribute generously. But in the ensuing years the primary leader, and undoubtedly the most eloquent and forceful of all its patrons, the President, Spencer H. Cone, believed that the restriction that the society concentrate on translations into foreign languages should be removed. He believed that the *Authorized Version* — that is, the *King James Version*, noble and adequate as it was in most respects and sanctified by the high place it held in the English Bible tradition, had significant defects. He constantly lobbied for the new society to work towards producing a new translation in the English tongue which was more faithful to the original language.

At its annual meeting on 11 May 1849, twelve years after it was launched in Philadelphia, the society presented a resolution, largely through Spencer Cone's influence no doubt, that the previous policy of using only the commonly received version of the Bible should be removed. This meant that the *Authorized Version*, the *King James Version*, hoary with tradition and beloved by Christians of all denominations, was to be 'corrected'. Spencer Cone was to learn, what many since have also learned to their great grief and suffering, that in the eyes of many people tampering with this version of the Bible is a cardinal sin.

Along with the resolution of the majority of the American and Foreign Bible Society which called for a new English version, a minority report was issued by Warren Carter, Esq. who argued at length that the common version was not to be altered at all. Carter, was one of the early '*King James* only' men who have since made such a noise throughout the English-speaking world. Carter was described by the historian Armitage as an intelligent man but one who was woefully lacking in the academic skills needed to enter this type of debate. Carter demanded that if the *KJV* was to be amended, the advocates of this change should submit specimens of their modifications. William Colgate approved of this suggestion and said that he, as a friend of the revision, would personally finance such an edition.

When the news of the proposed changes to the English version of the Bible and the objection to it began to spread throughout the Baptist churches of America, a fierce debate arose across the land and people everywhere began to take sides. Baptist journals were filled with articles both for and against on the subjects, and the pulpits thundered forth declamations of a similarly divided sentiment. Many denounced the new Bible society led by Cone as an apostate organization which was daring to corrupt the pure Word of God, that had been used by the godly for centuries. Others endorsed the society as simply desiring to strain out of the common translation corruptions that originated in the Episcopal prejudices of the scholars brought together by King James.

In the end the American and Foreign Bible Society decided that it was attempting something too big for it to accomplish. At the thirteenth anniversary of the society in New York, in a moment of high drama and excitement, with a huge crowd of life members present, the Convention was called upon to respond to a motion proposed by Rev. Robert Turnbull, pastor of the South Baptist Church in Hartford, Connecticut. It read: 'Resolved, that it is not the province and duty of the American and Foreign Bible Society to attempt, on their own part, or procure from others, a revision of the commonly received English version of the Scriptures.' The resolution was adopted by a vote of the delegates. When the time came to elect new officers, all the old managers, including the secretary, William H. Wyckoff, and William Colgate, the treasurer, were removed, the single exception was Spencer Cone who was once again elected as president. Although Cone, like Wyckoff, was opposed to the resolution, his lofty status carried him back into office.

Spencer Cone had been a friend of the cause of Bible translation and distribution from the earliest times of his ministry. He had nurtured the old American Bible Society in its infant days and had sadly parted with it when it was no longer able to use Baptist translators. For thirteen years he had been at the front of the new American and Foreign Bible Society, as it launched and sustained its many agencies in the mission fields of the world. In his own mind, at least, and indeed, in fact and reality, he had given the fullest of the energies of his manhood to the cause of the Bible societies. His church had hosted Bible Society conferences and he was always at the highest levels of leadership. The successes these societies had enjoyed were indebted to him in no small measure. But now the man, whose head was crowned with the snows of many winters, living in the twilight of his long and remarkable life, faced a terrible humiliation and defeat. His heart was broken and he saw no course for himself but resignation from the presidency.

Out of the conflict came a third Bible translation society, known as the American Bible Union, which was organized on the 10 June 1850 at the Baptist Tabernacle in Mulberry Street, New York. The old leadership of Cone, Wyckoff, and Colgate was transferred, almost automatically, to this new society. The stated purpose of the Union was the translation of the pure Word of God, not merely in foreign tongues but in English as well. Thus the Baptist denomination in America had two translation societies, one committed to doing a job on foreign soil only, and the other labouring to include English revision in its agenda. Distinguished leaders were involved in both organizations, but predictably, with such a serious rupture in the Baptist corpus, neither society made out very well financially. This unfortunate controversy was settled finally in May of 1883 when the whole matter of Bible translation was turned over to the American Baptist Publication Society and the American Baptist Missionary Union. The former was to take care of Bible work at home, while the latter was to attend to foreign distribution.

Arguably the issues involved in this Bible translation controversy were not of sufficient importance for such a violent division. One could wish, with hindsight, that the great gospel champion, Spencer Cone, had not been embroiled in this debate to the extent that he was, and had not sacrificed himself on this altar. After all, he had taken a neutral ground on the more important issue of the appointment of slave holders to the mission field. In many areas of theology, politics, and practical Christian endeavour he was for the most part moderate, flexible and given to peace. But on the question of the purity of the Bible, for him there could be no compromise. This was a hill he was willing to die on, and arguably that hill provided him his fatal wound.

16.

A confessional faith

It was a moment of high drama when the Baptist patriarch, Spencer Cone, resigned from the presidency of the American and Foreign Bible Society, gave his farewell speech, and walked out of the meeting followed by his compatriots, William Colgate and William Wyckoff. The scene is described by Thomas Armitage, the Baptist historian, who was at the meeting:

> No person then present can wish to witness another such scene in a Baptist body to the close of life. Dr Cone, at that time in his sixty-sixth year, rose like a patriarch, his hair as white as snow. As soon as the seething multitude in the Mulberry Street Tabernacle could be stilled, he said, with a stifled and almost choked utterance, 'Brethren, I believe my work in this society is done. Allow me to tender you my resignation. I did not withdraw my name in advance, because of the seeming egotism of such a step. I thank you, my brethren, for the kindly manner in which you have been pleased to tender me once more the office of president of your society. But I cannot serve you longer. I am crushed.' The society at first refused to receive his resignation, but, remaining firm in his purpose, it was accepted. When Messrs Cone, Colgate and Wyckoff rose to leave the house in company, Dr Cone invited Dr Sommers, the first vice-president, to the chair, remarking that God had a work for him to do which he was not permitted to do in that society; and

bowing, like a prince in Israel, uncrowned for his fidelity, he said amid the sobbing of the audience, 'I bid you, my brethren, an affectionate farewell as president of a society that I have loved which has cost me money, with much labour, prayer and tears. I hope that God will direct your future course in mercy; that we may do as much good as such creatures as we are able to accomplish. May the Lord bless you all.'[1]

The goal of the leaders of the American Bible Union, which was organized in the wake of the problems of American and Foreign Bible Society, was partially fulfilled following this painful separation, though not to the extent of the vision of Spencer Cone. In 1851 a version edited by Cone and Wyckoff, entitled 'The commonly received version of the New Testament of our Lord and Savior, With Several Hundred Emendations', was published. In the introduction to that work the stated purpose is given: 'This book is designed for the examination of the members of the American and Foreign Bible Society, to convince them that the common version can be corrected without injury to its characteristic excellencies, and with great enhancement of its real value.'[2] It translates Matthew 28:19 as follows: 'Go ye therefore, and disciple all nations, immersing them into the name of the Father, and of the Son, and of the Holy Spirit.' In 1892 the American Baptist Publication Society, which had inherited and was still committed to the mission of the American Bible Union, also printed an 'improved' version of the New Testament.

These efforts to amend the *Authorized Version* of the Bible essentially failed, in so far as establishing commonly used versions which translated baptism by the word immersion. But it can be said that Baptist leaders since then have had no problem teaching their view of the holy ordinance of baptism from the *Authorized Version*, or any other of the more recent versions, from the *English Revised* to the *New International Version*.

To a Baptist, even without such a direct help as that which Cone and company sought to give, the meaning of baptism is evident from the original definition of 'baptizo' (which can be explained every time the subject is addressed), the symbolism of the ordinance, and the circumstantial evidence in the New Testament that baptism was administered to believers by their being dipped.

Baptists today can only admire the conviction, courage and faithfulness of the men who fought so valiantly for a translation which accurately conveyed the original meaning of baptism. But they would disagree, for the most part, with Cone, Wyckoff and their friends when they argue in the 'Principles and Intention of the American Bible Union' that the distinction between essentials and non-essentials in matter of duty is 'infidel'.[3] Were such a view upheld consistently there could never be a denomination, church or any Christian society which could have internal harmony, for it would be difficult, if not impossible, to find two independent, thinking people, Baptists or otherwise, who agreed on *everything*. History, it seems, has decreed that Christians teach their particular views on the ordinance of baptism from editions of the Bible which *transfer*, rather than translate, the Greek words.

Cone's failure to carry the American and Foreign Bible Society in the translation controversy temporarily retarded and discouraged him in his pursuit of the causes he believed in, but he was by no means totally stymied by this. Although somewhat alienated from his Baptist brethren who took a more accommodating position on Bible translations, he found in the First Baptist Church of New York and the American Bible Union many platforms from which he could proclaim the gospel as he understood it and contend for his convictions. His church loved him, prayed for him, and held him up in all the battles, struggles, and trials of his latter days. The erection of the commodious new church in the winter of 1842 opened many opportunities for outreach for the congregation which had just recently come through such turbulent times. In seven years the membership of the church grew from 200 to 600, the largest so far in its history. The bond between the pastor and his people was strong. The shepherd fed them week after week from the Word of truth and protected them from the devouring wolves of theological error and moral dissipation. The flock eagerly absorbed and grew under his teaching, and rallied around him as enemies rose to challenge his unflinching fidelity to the cause of Christ.

> In truth, pastor and people were fitted to each other by a nicer than human cunning. God touched their hearts together, with the coals from off his altar, and kindled between them an equal flame of ardor in his service, and loving confidence in each other. Their pastor loved them with all the general warmth and strong passion of his nature, and they returned his affection an hundred fold into his own bosom. They understood and appreciated him, and he felt and knew it. They were, in his own language, 'a lovely church' to him, strong in doctrine, ardent in the Lord's work, and the fear of man was not upon them... When he was in trouble, they sought him; when his enemies raged against him, they defended him, and were as a living wall about him.[4]

When Cone came to the First Baptist Church in 1841, he found the congregation established firmly on the truths of the Bible as understood by the Particular Baptists of Great Britain and America. Their doctrines were outlined in the records of the church and appeal was made to the 'scriptures as a whole' for proof of these views. But their pastor noted that, as yet, they had not articulated these teachings in a formal way through any confessional summary. This deficiency he was determined to correct. He immediately set about to draw up a confession of faith which could embody the convictions of his congregation.

Had he wished, he could have proposed to the congregation the famous *Philadelphia Confession* of 1742, which was a slight modification of the old *Second London Confession* of 1689. He could have used the *New Hampshire Confession* of 1833, although this confession was not widely known at the time. It became popular later when in 1853 J. Newton Brown, editorial secretary of the American Baptist Publication Society, revised and printed it.

There is no evidence that Cone bothered to research previous confessions, or borrow from them extensively, as he proceeded to lead his congregation to a more specific and biblically-supported statement of faith. Instead, assisted no doubt by other like-minded brethren, he composed and proposed an original confession admirable for its orthodoxy, simplicity and clarity. At a regularly scheduled meeting of the church on 28 July 1841, the church adopted the 'Summary of Faith and Practice', which also included a church covenant. It consists of twenty articles which did not differ in the least from the truths contained in other more widely used confessions characteristic of Calvinistic Baptists. On the doctrine of the Trinity it says, 'We believe that there is *one*, and but *one living and true god*, who subsisteth in *three equal persons*: the *Father*, the *Son* and *Holy Spirit*.' On man's depravity it states: 'That all mankind, *by nature*, are totally and universally depraved, and therefore without either ability or inclination to return to God, or to render perfect obedience to his moral requirements.' On the authority of Scripture, election, atonement, regeneration, heaven and hell, and all the other truths proclaimed by the Regular Baptist Churches, it hues the line.[5]

The 'Summary of Faith and Practice' is remarkable for its clarity, brevity, simplicity and faithfulness to the Word of God. One can easily imagine the author of this admirable document adopting the words of the chief Musician, who penned Psalm 45. 'My heart is inditing a good matter: I speak of the things which I have made touching the king: my tongue is the pen of a ready writer' (v. 1). The statement of faith of the First Baptist Church formed a bulwark against error for this congregation, steered them through many turbulent conflicts in the spiritual battles of the day, and adequately expressed their views on the Christian faith. Spencer Cone saw no contradiction between a solid doctrinal foundation and true devotion to God and service for him. In fact, he believed that one formed the basis of the other. For him piety could not flow properly without being guided by the banks of biblical truth. The faith of pastor, deacons, and members of the church was confessional, rational and uncompromising.

The 'Summary', in common with most regularly constituted Baptist Churches of the period, affirmed the doctrine of closed communion, as opposed to open communion. This view supports the practice of limiting the distribution of the elements of the Lord's Supper in Baptist churches exclusively to those who have been immersed. It states in section 18: 'We also believe that subjection to baptism is prerequisite to admission into a visible church, and therefore, to partaking of the Lord's Supper.' This viewpoint was then, as indeed it still is today, controversial and offensive toPaedobaptists who felt disenfranchised because they were not invited to commune with the Baptists at the Lord's table. But in the eyes of the Baptists of this period, their views on the Lord's Supper were not a repudiation of the sincere Christian profession of their Methodist or Presbyterian brethren, or any others who gave evidence of love for the Saviour. They were only carrying out in a logical way their conviction that in the divine order baptism must precede communion, and since baptism is only by immersion that excluded the Paedobaptists. Obviously, they distinguished Christian fellowship from church fellowship.

The 'Summary' also has a stronger than usual statement on the separation of Church and State, which reflected the unshakable conviction of its author: '...we believe that the kingdom of Christ is not of this world; that the gospel church, therefore, is neither national nor parochial, and that none belong to her by virtue of their natural descent from her members. A visible gospel church should consist of such persons only as make a credible profession of faith in Christ, receive his gospel and obey his precepts.' The sentiments in this section had been hammered out by the Baptists through many centuries of trial and fire, and Spencer Cone insisted that they be articulated very specifically. For these Christians the church is a body of faithful believers, not believers and their children. And clearly the notion that a person becomes a member of a national church simply by being born into that community was regarded as an abomination. Jonathan Edwards repudiated the 'half-way covenant' view that the ordinances of the church can be a means of conversion, and he suffered for this stand. But Spencer Cone and the Baptists went a step further and insisted that the sacred ordinances of baptism and the Lord's Supper must be administered only to those who give a clear testimony of conversion. Cone would have argued that the Baptists were taking the doctrine of *Sola Scriptura* of the Protestant Reformation to its logical conclusion by forbidding the admission of any except believers to the sacred ordinances of baptism (by immersion) and the Lord's Supper.

Spencer Cone built upon the solid doctrinal foundation of the First Baptist Church a dynamic, evangelistic, progressive ministry. The beautiful new building was occupied in 1842, and, through the insistence of the pastor, was home to the American and Foreign Bible Society and the American Home Mission Society of his denomination. The cause of leading lost sinners to God was constantly pressed upon the consciences of the members, and from that congregation, through every means at their disposal, the gospel light was beamed forth to all the world.

Cone had been a prime agent in the vision of world-wide missions which had activated the Baptist denomination for many decades. In a letter to R. E. Pattison, corresponding secretary of the Missionary Union in 1844, he confessed, 'The work and cause of missions must be the business of my life.' The First Baptist Church was at once a nursery of missionary enterprise and a haven for preachers of the Word of God, whether labouring on foreign or domestic fields. The pastor sponsored and entertained missionaries, raised money, and promoted their interests from his pulpit. His children witnessed first-hand, day by day, the passion he had for evangelistic causes, as demonstrated in his fervent prayers in the domestic circle. He had, of course, a special burden for his own beloved land of America. 'He never bent his knee at the family altar without praying for his native land, as a child might pray for a parent tenderly beloved.'

The First Baptist Church was one that bore lasting fruit in its multiplied influence. Like the Metropolitan Tabernacle under the leadership of Charles Spurgeon, it was instrumental in the founding of many other churches of like faith. Second Baptist, Bethel Baptist, Zoar, Abyssinian, Peekskill, North, Stamford, and Bethesda were only a few new churches planted under the sponsorship of this congregation. Among the ministers sent out were: Thomas Ustic, Ebenezer Ferris, Isaac Skillman, Stephen Gano, Thomas Montayne, Cornelius P. Wyckoff, James Bruce, John Seger, Simeon J. Drake, William Rollinson, Henry C. Fish, Solomon Relyea, and Thomas T. Devan. Biographical summaries of Ustic, Gano, Montayne, Wyckoff, Seger, Drake, Fish, Relvea and Devan can be found in the *Baptist Encyclopedia* of 1881. Fish was a noted author, famous especially for his *Pulpit Eloquence of the Nineteenth Century*. Devan, who joined the First Baptist Church under the ministry of Cone, was a missionary for a while in China and eventually in France.

*Picture of Spencer Cone in the great hall
of the First Baptist Church*

17.

A powerful pen

From his earliest efforts at public preaching, Spencer Cone exhibited a natural gift for preaching. With a voice, which Thomas Armitage described as 'rich, powerful and melodious,' with a heart which was warmed by an earnest love for God and stirred by deep compassion for his fellow man, and with a mind remarkably gifted for memory, his ability to influence men from the pulpit was legendary. Gifted with a mind approaching photographic capabilities, he was able to preach without notes. One disadvantage, however, attended this ability, and that was that he left behind very little by way of printed texts of his sermons. These powerful messages, carefully prepared but delivered without any manuscripts, turned hundreds to God and stirred the souls of believers. They are, unfortunately, lost for ever. In reviewing this remarkable man, we can only regret that he did not take the time to enlist the services of a person who could have at least recorded the essence of his messages in writing.

However, we do have excellent examples of his writing skills, not in the form of entire books which he composed, but in articles and essays on various subjects. The well-written 'Summary' of the doctrines of the First Baptist Church exhibits not only his comprehensive grasp of truth but also his gift for precise expression. His printed writings include introductions to biographical works, such as that of the Baptist apologist, Rev. William Judd, articles written in defence of correct Bible translations and the 'Principles and Intentions of the American Bible Union'. Perhaps his character as a thinker and his incisiveness as a communicator on theoretical and practical divinity can best be seen, however, in the circular letters he composed for distribution among the churches in the Baptist Associations of which he was a part.

The first attempt of Baptists to cooperate together and coordinate their efforts in common causes took the form of the Baptist Association. Long before there was any attempt at a national missionary society, such as the Trienniel Convention of 1814, Baptists in all parts of the country formed associations in their own vicinity. The prototype of the Association, indeed the first of its kind on the North American Continent, was the Philadelphia Baptist Association which was formed in 1707 from five small churches in the Delaware Valley. The Association grew with the young nation and, at one time, extended as far as Virginia and New York, covering a 400 mile span.

For at least the first 150 years of its existence in Baptist life, the Association was the primary agency through which Baptists defined themselves as a people, cooperated in missions, and preserved their theological integrity. Were one to attend one of the annual meetings of any of these bodies in the eighteenth or throughout most of the nineteenth century, in addition to the usual statistical summaries and reports that necessarily attend such gatherings, one would have heard debates about intricate points of doctrine and practice. The conclusions were printed in the annual minutes of the Association annual meeting and distributed as a 'Circular Letter'.

The profound theological and spiritual sensitivities of these Baptists can be seen by the topics that were addressed in the 'Circular Letters' of the Philadelphia Association. Their policies and practices were adopted by other such bodies which were organized at a later stage. The minutes from 1707 to 1807 of this pristine Baptist body in America were printed by the

Association in 1851 and edited by A. D. Gillette, a close friend
of Spencer Cone and pastor of the Eleventh Baptist Church of
Philadelphia. Subjects of these letters included the great themes
of the gospel, such as the Trinity, the decrees and perfections of
God, justification, adoption, effectual calling, assurance of salvation, the law of God, Christ's work as the Mediator and the
fall of man. Views on practical issues were promulgated, such
as fasting and prayer, the terms of communion, spiritual unity,
temperance, the political foundations of America, whether
women should be allowed to vote and the qualifications of a
minister.

The churches of which Spencer Cone was pastor for the
final thirty-four years of his life belonged to the New York Baptist Association. He was often called upon to give the doctrinal
sermons at the conventions and he was also asked to put them
in written form to be issued as annual circular letters. Indeed, it
mattered not what body he became a part of, be it a society to
promote missions, or provide biblical versions, or direct the
course of denominational affairs, he always seemed to be
regarded as the most capable thinker and spokesman. The minutes of the New York Association reveal that he spoke and wrote
on such subjects as the qualifications for partaking of communion
and the need for a correct Bible translation. Two articles of
special interest are 'The Work of the Holy Spirit' and 'The Restoration of the Jews'. These deserve special attention for they exhibit eminently the exegetical techniques, theological convictions and literary style of their author.

The fifty-sixth anniversary of the New York Baptist Association was held at the First Baptist Church of New York on Tuesday and Wednesday, 26 and 27 May 1846. The 'Circular Letter',
which was incorporated into the published minutes, was sent
to all the churches, along with a 'Christian salutation'. Like the
letters of Paul these epistles were intended to instruct and edify
the members of the church, though not to impose some hard

and fast creed upon them. Spencer Cone composed the letter, addressing the constituents as 'Dearly beloved in the Lord'. The subject, 'The Work of the Holy Spirit', is divided into five sections: the work of the Spirit is free; the work of the Spirit is necessary; the work of the Spirit is almighty; the work of the Spirit is definite; and the work of the Holy Spirit is holy. There is nothing in this document that would have seemed strange to a member of one of the Particular Baptist Churches in the mid-nineteenth century, but a modern delegate to a typical Baptist Association in any one of the major groups would undoubtedly scratch his head in amazement at some of the sentiments.

On the subject of the freeness of the work of the Holy Spirit, Cone affirmed the absolute right of God as the Sovereign of the universe to bestow his grace on whomever he wishes. Basing his position on such texts as 'He doth his pleasure in heaven and on earth; he giveth and he taketh away; he killeth and he maketh alive, and none can say what does thou?', he shuts the sinner up to the agency of God for deliverance from the bondage of sin:

> As an independent Sovereign, *he giveth no account of any of his matters,* but dispenseth his saving benefits upon whomsoever he pleaseth, nor does Gabriel ask the reason why, or God the reason give. As a Sovereign he is under no obligation to angels who have kept their first estate; much less can he be under obligation to confer happiness upon worms of the dust who have rebelled against his righteous government, and violated his law, which is holy, just and good... Man is totally depraved — *the whole head is sick, and the whole heart is faint.* If left to ourselves, we should never will to run in the right ways of the Lord: but it is all of mercy, therefore that he hath willed the salvation of any; and if we are permitted to enjoy a good hope of *obtaining that salvation which is in Christ Jesus, with eternal glory,* we must ascribe it to the will of him, whose counsel shall stand, and who will do all his pleasure.[1]

The writer of these lines was the pastor of the one of the largest and most prestigious Baptist churches in America. For nine consecutive years he was elected president of the Baptist Trienniel Convention, the first agency of Baptists in America to promote foreign missions. He served many years as corresponding secretary of the New York Baptist Domestic Missionary Society, and was twelve years chairman of the Executive Board of the American Baptist Home Mission Society. He did not regard adherence to a high Calvinism as being inimical to an aggressive missionary vision. Undergirding his dynamic leadership, supporting his vision and energizing his motivations was a belief that God can save whom he will.

The drift of Baptists in America from Calvinism to Arminianism, and eventually to a virtual Pelagianism is a historical tragedy of which all Baptists who are interested in their theological traditions should be aware. Admittedly there has been a division of Baptists on the Calvinist-Arminian controversy from the times of the earliest settlers in America. But the beginnings of a humanistic approach to bring men to God can essentially be traced to the theology of Charles G. Finney who first popularized the idea that the natural man has the power to convert himself. It was he who introduced methods in evangelism which focused on manipulating unconverted men to make decisions in public meetings. The popular doctrine, usually preached and taught in the majority of Baptist churches in America, is that while the Holy Spirit must move upon the hearts of men, convicting them of sin and assisting them towards a decision for Christ, ultimately it is the sinner who makes himself to differ in the matter of conversion. A typical evangelical or fundamentalist type Baptist at the beginning of the twenty-first century would affirm without question that man is a sinner in need of repentance who must turn to Christ. But the idea that the sinner's alienation from God is so desperate and drastic that in sovereign, electing grace God must move to change him is repudiated with disgust.[2]

Thomas Armitage (1819-1889), the Baptist historian, was a young admirer of Spencer Cone. He was thirty-one when the violent rupture took place in the American and Foreign Bible Society and he thoroughly sympathized with Cone in that controversy. In fact, he became president of the American Bible Union himself in 1856. He was called upon to be the primary preacher at the funeral of his beloved mentor, and candour demanded that he comment on Cone's Calvinism. 'From the early part of his ministry,' he said, '[Cone] made himself perfect master of the writings of Thomas Scott, Matthew Henry, Abraham Booth, Jonathan Edwards, John Gill, John Owen and John Calvin. More than all else, he read and studied the Word of God; its prayerful perusal being a part of his daily meat and drink, to the end of his life.'[3] The writers mentioned here were all well known by the leading Baptist pastors of this era.

Armitage summarized the Calvinist convictions of the New York pastor in his funeral address. Undoubtedly, the great crowd that thronged the meeting house that day nodded in approval as he said:

On this principle he was a Calvinist, a Calvinist of the old school, and felt no apology necessary for being so. In preaching the distinctive doctrines of that school, he suffered no Antinomian sin to rest easy on any man; but enforced all the duties of the Christian life, by weighty motives and considerations. By his commission from Christ, he aimed to awaken the secure — to quicken the slothful — to strengthen the weak — and to warn the rebellious to 'flee from the wrath to come.' ...Nor did he think it necessary, in preaching these and their correlative truths, to apologize for the mysteries of the gospel, in a fruitless attempt to level them to the claims of reason. Herein he 'showed himself a workman that needed not to be ashamed, rightly dividing the word of truth'. Reason revolts at the doctrine of the moral agency of man, being coupled as it is with that of the sovereignty of Jehovah in his salvation. But what then?

Are we at liberty to reject either of these doctrines of the Bible
for this cause. I think not.[4]

Armitage was pointing out that the twin doctrines of human
free agency and God's absolute sovereignty are both taught in
the Word of God. Cone believed and preached both, although
in the minds of men they seem contradictory. In his message,
Armitage goes on to show that there are other mysteries of
divine revelation, such as the *unity* of God in *three* persons and
the one undivided nature of Jesus Christ who is *both* God and
man. In 1855 a gathering of mourners at the funeral of an eminent minister would not have thought it strange that the preacher
elaborated on the theological views of the deceased, even giving
a polemic in their defence.

Cone's article on 'The Restoration of the Jews' was printed
as a 'Circular Letter' of the New York Association for the year
1844. He begins by expressing his surprise that the Association,
which had been organized in 1791, had dealt with 'almost every
other doctrine and duty' in their confession, but had neglected
this subject. 'Why?' he asked. Not, he assures us, because the
Scriptures are silent upon the subject. He hints that one cause
may have been a latent anti-Semitism. 'Have we lived under
the influence of that baleful prejudice which has so long shut up
the tender mercies of the rest of the human family towards them,
and which has seemed to grudge them even the sympathy of a
tear?'[5]

Cone's primary line of argument is from the texts of Scripture which, from all appearance, predict a regathering and conversion of God's ancient people, Israel. He cites many passages, not only from the pre-exilic prophets such as Isaiah,
Jeremiah and Amos, but also Ezekiel who prophesied during
the exile and Zechariah who prophesied after the exile. He
quotes Zechariah 10:6 which says, 'And I will strengthen the
house of Judah, and I will save the house of Joseph, and I will

bring them again to place them; for I have mercy upon them: and they shall be as though I had not cast them off: for I am the Lord their God, and will hear them.' 'This occurrence,' he notes, 'has not yet taken place.'

Cone argues also from the amazing continuance of the Jewish people as a national and cultural entity, in spite of not having a homeland for so long:

> Our views upon this subject are yet more confirmed by their miraculous preservation. Although scattered among all nations, the Jews remain a distinct people; it is the wonder of the world: 'the observed of all observers'. Other nations more numerous and more powerful, have either melted away entirely, or have been lost in the general mass of mankind: while *they stand alone,* like a rock in the ocean, unmingled with the surrounding waters, reserved by divine providence to display the glory of Israel's God in the *restoration* of this favored nation.[6]

He advances another argument which is not often used, even by those who agree with his views on this subject. Israel must return and be restored to their homeland, he contends, because they are a *typical people*, and to be a true type they must illustrate the unchanging and infallible promises of God. Spiritual Israel, the true redeemed family of God, is secured in its perseverance from 'grace to glory', and so physical Israel, which pictures this covenant-keeping grace of God, must enjoy the same divine mercy in their ultimate national recovery. 'Our argument is that if spiritual Israel on the ground of Jehovah's promise, shall possess for ever the heavenly Canaan, "the rest that remaineth for the people of God", then this glorious truth is only adequately shadowed forth by the literal restoration of national Israel to the earthly Canaan; and the one can no more fail than the other.'[7] Cone argued that the promises of God which relate to physical or earthly blessings, such as his covenant with Noah not to destroy the earth by water, are just as certain as the promises that relate to spiritual blessings. The same immutable character of God is engaged in both types of promises.

Cone was aware that 'many good men' argue that the promises that appear to relate to the nation Israel are fulfilled spiritually in the church. But, he contends, this line of reasoning would cast doubt upon all the prophecies of God which related to his purposes in the world. God's promise to give Abraham a son, his promise to bring Israel back after seventy years captivity and his promise that the Messiah would be born of a virgin, 'all these, and many other promises were literally fulfilled,' so why should the promises relating to Israel's national revival and conversion be spiritualized?

Cone clearly had no doubt, based on the promises of the Bible, that God had an infallible plan that includes the regathering and re-establishment of Israel as a homeland. He propounded these views at a time when the prospects of a national life of Israel in Palestine were totally without any visible probability. The Zionist movement began some fifty years after Cone made known his views, and Israel's rebirth under the auspices of the United Nations was over one hundred years later. But the New York pastor had a child-like faith in the Word of God and took its prophecies literally, regardless of any difficulties that seemed to lie in the way of their fulfilment. He would not have been surprised when in May 1948 this little nation was dug out of the Arab world, in the most unfavourable circumstances, and with great cost to its peoples.

18.

Counselling young ministers

Like many other great ministers, such as George Whitefield, Charles Spurgeon, and Benajah H. Carroll, Cone was unquestionably a model for young men entering into the ministry. Although he never taught in a seminary — in fact, he never attended a theological school — his many preaching opportunities in various settings exposed him to the attention of men preparing to preach themselves. They were inspired by his earnestness, encouraged by his boldness and strengthened by his convictions. As he grew older, they went to him for counsel and advice. He had a great interest in helping young preachers and devoted a lot of his time to instructing them.

He left behind no manual for preparation for the pulpit or lectures on homiletics, but his biographers observed and recorded his words of encouragement and counsel to young preachers. Also, he was a busy and voluminous letter writer, and some of his correspondents made available these epistles in which he poured out his soul to them and urged them on in their work. One such beneficiary of his written counsels was John Wesley Sarles, whom he baptized at the Oliver Street Church on 5 April 1835. Sarles became a very successful minister himself, pastoring the Central Baptist Church of Brooklyn, New York where he remained for thirty-two years. The letters from Cone to Sarles provided for his biographers, and for us, the fruit of his thinking on the proper methods of the preacher.

Preparation for the pulpit

Cone advocated and practised in his own life the principle that
preparation for the pulpit is a continual business. Although he
was an avid reader, he did not believe that preparation for
preaching takes place solely in the study. His school was life
itself, the constant observation of events around him, whatever
the context, be it political, scientific, economic, social or religious. He believed that thinking and meditation were even
more important than reading. He said once, 'The man who
reads two hours and thinks six is the preacher I should like to sit
under.' Preaching the gospel for him was not merely a com-
partment of his life, it was the constant pursuit of every waking
moment, either in planning what to preach, delivering God's
Word from the pulpit, or reflecting on what he had said and the
results.

> He was always studying; and what he learned once he never
> forgot. He was always revolving in his mind some doctrine, or
> passage of scripture, or peculiarity of Christian experience, or
> great principles. Pass his study door, at any hour, and you would
> hear him talking over one or the other with himself. Hardly
> anything that passed about him in the world, escaped him;
> changes in government, political events in various countries,
> incidents and facts observed during his pastoral visits, remark-
> able discoveries in science were all seized by him and trans-
> muted by a happy mental alchemy into apt and striking illus-
> trations of some view of divine truth. It is impossible to tell
> exactly when or where men of this quality of mind study. They
> are studying you whilst they talk with you about the common-
> est things... The world, life, all that any sense can reach are
> hourly teachers of their thoughts, and fill them with the wisdom
> of which books may be made, but which they cannot teach.

He has often told us that he had never passed an idle hour from the time he was fourteen years old.[1]

Spencer Cone was a preacher every moment of his life. Whether he was travelling through the countryside, relaxing in the fellowship of his beloved wife, romping with his children or grandchildren, or pouring over some theological tome, he was learning about men and things, and making himself ready for the pulpit.

Primary themes for preaching

As we have seen already, Spencer Cone was thoroughly convinced of the trustworthiness of God's Word and was committed to the evangelical Baptist faith. He believed that man was a fallen sinner, totally shut up to the grace of God for any hope of redemption. He believed and preached the absolute necessity of a radical change of regeneration before anyone could claim to be a Christian or admitted into the church. For him judgement, heaven and hell were solemn realities to be kept constantly before his hearers. He insisted that the way of salvation for perishing sinners be included in every sermon. To Sarles he said, 'Accustom yourself to give Christ his place in every sermon. Get the gospel by the handle. Never preach a sermon without enough of the gospel to show a sinner how he must be saved.' And again, 'Whenever and wherever you preach, preach Christ. Never leave out Christ when you are trying to make in your thoughts the skeleton of a sermon. Habituate yourself to give him his place whatever be your subject.'[2] Spencer Cone believed that only Christ could save and that only by setting him forth in all his offices could mankind come to saving faith. A missionary to Ireland remarked of him, 'The great characteristics of his heart and mind seemed to be an invincible desire to set forth the gospel in all its heavenly light, linked with an unquenchable thirst for the salvation of men.'[3]

Learning to preach by preaching

Many in Cone's day, just as in ours, were convinced that several long years of academic discipline and spiritual development are necessary before a man should attempt to preach. But he believed that preaching can only be learned by doing. He himself was forced, as it were, into public ministry by necessity. Shortly after he was converted his gifts as a teacher and proclaimer of the Word were sought, and though 'fearing and trembling' at his own inadequacies, he proceeded to try and God blessed him. His recommendations to Sarles bear testimony to this point:

> You may sometimes be mortified and shut up, as others have been before you, but notwithstanding all this, preach *frequently*. Practice only makes perfect. A man might read about cutting out a coat until he was grey, and not be able to make a garment that would fit a lap-board after all. You must practice. Learn a little, and preach it; learn a little more and preach that, and so on, till you have the bag of the gospel, full of milk, to resort to, and your hand so thoroughly practiced in the art of milking, that you can pull away at the teat of election, and if the milk does not run freely, by the teat of adoption, or justification, or sanctification, or conversion, the offices of Christ, or the graces of the spirit, or the duties and privileges of the Christian, etc.[4]

Preaching extemporaneously

Cone believed that a Baptist preacher should be able to preach, 'at the drop of a hat', as it were. To Sarles he said, 'Why a Baptist preacher ought to be ready to preach at a minute's warning, if necessary.' He felt that the man of God should have a subject thoroughly thought out so that he could deliver it well at any time, with the help of the Lord. 'No, this is the motto for my preacher, *semper paratus*, and that the motto may be appropriate, let him remember that preaching is his business — his reasonable and delightful service.'

Cone thought that it was inappropriate for a minister to go into the pulpit with such a carefully prepared text that there was no room for the Holy Spirit to give immediate inspiration and illustration. He compared the office of the preacher to that of a lawyer pleading the cause of his client in court. The attorney is impressed with a due sense of the importance of his mission. His own reputation is at stake, and, even more importantly, the property, safety, and perhaps even the life of his client are on the line. The judge upon the bench and the jury in the box have the fate of the client in their hands. It is his job to convince them and present arguments with such power and persuasion that they will think like he wants them to think. It would leave a bad impression if he were to stand before a jury reading monotonously from a paper:

> To what a task does a good counsel set himself. Every power of the body, every quality of the mind is taxed and strained to the utmost. His memory contributes its stores of learning. His rhetoric adorns what is dry, smooths what is ragged, and makes the path so pleasant that his hearers are enticed with him wherever he will have them to. His fancy and imagination play with seductive brilliancy around the subject. His heart contributes

all its tenderest emotions to heighten and fix the impression, and stamp his words with the mint-mark of nature and truth. Does he not deserve success in a good cause?[5]

The application of this eloquent description of the defender in court to the minister of the gospel is plain enough. The preacher stands not before a black-robed judge who himself is a sinner but before the Supreme Creator, before whose eyes all men's lives are an open book. At stake is not merely temporary gain or loss but eternal salvation or damnation.

The preacher who is to plead with sinners; who is to stand between the living and the dead; who is to warn a soul worth more than all the worlds to flee from the wrath to come; who is to point him to Christ as the only Saviour for one so lost and guilty, the only Advocate with the Father; who is to endeavor to strike through the iron casing which bars the passage to his heart and arouse him to the imminent peril in which he stands; the man who is to tell that wonderful, that soul-piercing and enrapturing story of the cross, reads it all from a well-written manuscript! Can that man's soul be lifted up to the mercy-seat as he does so?

Can his heart be bursting with agony and love for precious human souls, his eyes fountains of tears, his whole being wrapt and engaged in the sublime responsibility of his office? It is possible it may, but can sinners see it in his eyes and hear it in his voice? Can he forget himself — his mere words — everything but the infinite sorrow of a lost soul, the infinite love of a dying, risen, interceding Saviour? And will that be so palpable that conviction will strike the dullest? I cannot think it.[6]

Preaching and active endeavour

Some preachers conceive of the ministry as solely a moving back and forth between the cloisters of a private study and the pulpit. Not so with Cone; he was a man of affairs. He took a great interest in all aspects of community life and lent his hand to any cause he really believed in. His participation in the life of his denomination, especially its missionary agencies and the various translation societies, has already been noted. We have also seen that during the course of his career he served as a newspaper editor and a chaplain in Congress. He was one of the first patrons of the University of the City of New York (now CCNY), and was a member of the council. He was a member of the board of the Colonization Society of New York and one of its most popular speakers. He gave much of his time and thought to the Christian Alliance, an association formed in New York for the diffusion of knowledge among the downtrodden nations of Italy and central Europe.

Cone was no cold academic hiding away in the dim recesses of his library. He studied, he prayed, and he thought; but he was constantly a man of action.

> During his entire career as a pastor, he was eminently a worker. Constantly preaching, fulfilling a round of pastoral duties, and actively engaged in every benevolent enterprise, it was not possible for him to devote much time to the studies of the closet. It would, however, be a mistake to suppose that he was ever anything but a hard student. He was always studying; and what he learned he never forgot.[7]

Favourite authors

Spurgeon once observed that it takes a very arrogant man to believe that the only worthwhile thoughts come from his own brain. Some claim such originality that they profess never to study the views of other men or women, nor do they feel a need to consult commentaries. But foolish is the preacher who does not master the great preachers and authors who have laboured before him. A great leader once observed, 'I see further than most because I stand on the shoulders of giants.'

Cone urged young ministers to make the Bible itself the primary subject of study and meditation. 'Give yourself chiefly to the study of the Bible,' he wrote to Sarles. 'Preachers need to know everything,' he said. 'Let them begin with first principles, and go on to perfection, making the *Bible* their daily companion, and valuing learning of any and every kind, only as it helps to understand and explain the Bible.'[8] He encouraged them to read a little, get it in their heads and go out and preach it. '*Reading* makes a full preacher, *thinking* makes a wise one, and *speaking* a ready one,' he said. It is no wonder that a man so saturated with the Word of God, so full of living and observing the world about him, changed the lives of so many people by his preaching and teaching.

As far as human authors were concerned, his favourite was the English Baptist, Abraham Booth. He wrote to Sarles, 'Read Booth's *Reign of Grace*, carefully and critically. If you should commit it to memory, it would do you good to the day of your death. It would furnish your mind with an outline of the plan of redeeming mercy, so that you could not be taken by surprise, or find yourself incapable at any time of defending a scriptural position.' Here is his comment to Sarles on his favourite writers:

You ask for standard works — they are so numerous and so various in their excellence that I scarcely know where to begin. I prefer Abram Booth (sic), six volumes (eight volumes, London), to any other human writer. Gill, Hall, Fuller, Bunyan have much that is good, but some things to be guarded against. McLain on Hebrews, and Haldane on Romans, one volume, eight volumes. Each are studies. I prize Haldane above the rest as a commentator.[9]

Cone was an independent and highly original thinker and preacher. He gleaned from many sources, but his power lay in his familiarity with the Holy Scriptures. He was full of the Bible and when he opened his mouth to speak texts of the Bible rolled out. This method he recommended and modelled to his students. 'Study the Bible prayerfully; commit to memory striking passages, that you may be mighty in the Scriptures, and then your profiting will appear unto all men.'[10]

Spencer did all he could to instruct, encourage and motivate young ministers, but he never tried to dominate them or suppress their individuality. Perhaps it was for that reason that they felt so comfortable in his presence and repaired to him for counsel. He considered them fellow ambassadors, and treated them as such. Sarles comments:

I said fellow ambassadors, for though they were young, he drew no lines between himself and them, assumed no right to dictate, claimed no superiority, but having presented the result of his own experience, was sure to leave them unhampered, and free to dissent, if they could. In the youngest of his brethren he fully recognized the right to exercise their own judgment, all that was spread before by their seniors.[11]

Cone recognized that powerful preaching requires a combination of physical, mental and emotional assets. He encouraged his students to develop intellectually, becoming familiar with classic authors both secular and religious. But above all, he wanted to train men to be men of prayer and spirituality. He neither promoted nor practised what was becoming the vogue of the time — that is, an attempt towards preaching that has a certain literary elegance or studied classical style. He believed that the man of God should preach straight from the Bible and straight from a heart deeply in love with Jesus Christ. God blessed him with full churches and devoted hearers. Sarles said:

Long years since I often remarked that while many other ministers with whom I met, talked much and largely about literary studies, and taste and training, style of composition and elocution — excellence in those particulars upon which the educated world sits in judgment — he was always seeking to make a *scriptural* preacher, a *gospel* preacher, *a spiritually-minded* preacher.[12]

19.

Sally's homegoing

At the age of seventy Spencer Cone was the one of the elder statesmen of Baptists in the United States. He had been a prime mover in one of the most critical eras of the growing Baptist denomination in the country. He had helped to nurse the Trienniel Convention in the time of its infancy and had supported its world-wide missionary outreach through its formative years. He had taken a leading part in the Bible societies which were distributing the Word of God in many different languages. His strong hand had been at the helm as the Baptist movement sailed through the stormy seas of sectional division. His church continued to grow and lead souls to Christ in the commercial and cultural heart of America, New York City.

But time was taking its toll. He still had a full head of hair, but it was snow white. The clear blue eyes flashed as he preached and lifted up Christ as the Saviour of men, but they were encased in a brow wrinkled with age. His voice was still rich and full, but softened by a heart that was often broken. He was a general who still knew how to lead the godly in spiritual warfare, but scars were evident. Some of the battles he fought he won, some he lost. But though often disappointed and saddened, he was never bitter. Above all, he never compromised. In woe or in weal, in sunshine and rain, on the mountain and in the valley, his stayed true to his course. His head was 'bloodied but unbowed'.

The last two years of his life were taken up with dealing with severe trials. Very serious difficulties arose between the Baptist missionaries on the field and the executive officers of the board of the Baptist Convention. These conflicts were so great that many patrons of this missionary endeavour began to lose confidence in the cause, which had been launched with so much sacrifice and effort. The financial resources of the people on the foreign field were jeopardized. A serious breach in the fellowship of Baptists in the foreign and home missionary societies seemed imminent.

The people involved turned to Spencer Cone for help. People on all sides trusted him implicitly. The leaders at home who managed the society had confidence in his wisdom and insight. The missionaries knew that he had their good at heart and always looked to him for support.

On 15 May 1855 the board met in Chicago and engaged in many hours of fruitless discussion. Two days later the Union itself met with George Dixon Briggs, who had formerly been governor of the state of Massachusetts, serving as moderator. A retired missionary offered a resolution affirming that the 'control' of the missionary board 'has frequently been exercised with too little regard to the rights and feelings of the missionaries themselves.'[1] The resolution did not pass.

Spencer Cone, supported by Baron Stow, recommended to the Union that a committee be formed consisting of one representative from each home state in the home-field. To this committee 'all differences' were to be referred, and it was to give a 'patient and attentive hearing to all that shall be offered by all the parties interested'.[2] This suggestion (which he had proposed earlier in New York without success) was adopted with satisfactory results. 'The excitement was calmed, brethren reconciled, difficulties smoothed away, and the great cause of missions apparently rescued from danger.'[3]

All the parties involved recognized the great value of Cone's mediation in this dispute. A major catastrophe which could have derailed the whole cooperative Baptist missionary cause had been averted through his prudent intervention. One of those who recognized and applauded Cone's efforts was Governor Briggs. Writing to his biographers, he said, 'I am quite sure, if all of us members of the American Baptist Missionary Union, and its missions, upon whom rests the responsibility of settling the disagreeable differences which were the subject of the proposition of our departed friend and brother, could be actuated by that spirit which actuated him on that occasion, those differences would not long remain as obstructions in our path of duty, and in our course of usefulness.'[4]

The speeches of Cone at the missionary conference in Chicago were, as Briggs noted, the 'last acts and last words' of Spencer Cone at an association of his assembled brethren. Briggs knew from the appearance and demeanour of the great leader that his days among them were numbered. His description of Cone leaves no doubt that this was the case: 'His pale face, his emaciated and feeble frame, the unnatural brilliancy of his fine eye, and the softened tones of his clear voice, were to me so many melancholy witnesses that we were looking upon him, and listening to him for the last time. I know that others concurred with me in these gloomy forebodings. Death had set a seal upon him, and the news that so soon followed, that death had smitten his own victim, was not surprising.'[5]

If we go back a few months we can better understand why Cone had declined in health and vigour in the year 1855. At the time of his long trip to Chicago he was a widower, for his beloved wife, Sally, had died the previous August. Never a robust person, her delicate constitution had not adjusted to the northern climate. She had been constantly plagued with respiratory problems since their move from Virginia. Often during the winter months she was taken South when her health warranted travel.

Her final days were spent in a resort area in northwestern New Jersey called Schooley's Mountain. From the time when the first settlers came to this area, now known as Washington Township, it was famous for its pure mountain air and romantic surroundings. In 1815 the mineral spring was declared to be the purest and best chalybeate water known in America. First discovered by the Lenape Indians, the waters were thought to have healing powers from the iron deposits found in the nearby mountains. Attracted by the peaceful environs and restorative waters, people came by the thousands to retire from the heat of the summers in the cities on the Eastern seaboard. The old hotel register in Washington Township shows that a large number of distinguished guests, including visitors from Philadelphia, Baltimore, Charleston and other distant parts of the country, came there to drink and bath in the waters.[6] Spencer and Sally Cone were among such visitors.

Here in this secluded and peaceful spot the devoted pair came to rest, meditate and refresh their spirits. In Schooley's Mountain they could get away from the hustle and bustle of city life and reflect upon the greatness and glory of their God and Redeemer. While staying in their own special room, with a privacy which all around them respected, they would study, pray and plan for the many engagements which filled their lives in New York. Here Spencer was freed from the interruptions of his home on Broome Street. He always took along with him the numerous volumes which provided his intellectual and spiritual challenges of the moment. He planned the agenda of the agencies he managed, prepared sermons and engaged in his extensive correspondence.

When tired of reading or writing he would stroll up and down the piazza of the hotel and gaze upon the beautiful hills in the distance. Especially enjoyable were the walks he and his inseparable companion would take, arm in arm, through the wooded paths along the plateau and up to the mountain top. Here, according to his sons, he had a particular spot where he came to watch the ending of the day. From this place the last rays of the sun could be seen colouring the 'undulating hills' to the west, with their shadows darkening the deep valley below. Here he would stand, often alone, for an hour or more watching the glories of the sunset. As the crimson and gold faded into the grey of twilight, he seemed lost in quiet and heavenly contemplation. What profound thoughts, what powerful sermons, what lofty and noble enterprises must have filled his heart in these moments. The children of Israel had their Elim, and Cone had his Schooley's Mountain. Happy is the Christian who can find such a place where, in deep solitude and silence, he can worship the Creator and ponder the meaning of life.

While residing briefly in their favourite place of retreat in Schooley's Mountain, the family and friends of Spencer Cone were able to learn even more about the depth of his life of personal faith and devotion. When visitors knew that he was there, he would hold conferences for spiritual exhortation and prayer. They were often invited in and, in many instances, heard the gospel of Christ for the first time, since his public prayers were always full of the Redeemer. 'Many men and women kneeled and listened there to what they had perhaps never heard before, for in his public prayers, as in his sermons, the way of salvation for sinners through the alone merits sake of the blood of Christ (sic) was very plainly preached.'[7] Perhaps the Christian and the preacher especially can learn something of the secret of the energy that often is given to a servant of Jesus. Like Jesus who often abandoned his busy career of preaching and ministering to go into the mountains to pray, Cone found spiritual renewal in prayer.

Like the setting sun which they often watched as it fell behind the New Jersey mountains, the lives of Spencer and Sally Cone, in so far as their earthly pilgrimage was concerned, were coming to an end as the middle of the nineteenth century passed. In August of 1854 they took their accustomed trip to Schooley's mountain to escape the stifling heat of the inner-city of New York. Sally had suffered for five years with ulcers of the mouth and tongue and looked, as usual, for a cure, or at least some relief, in the clear mountain air and the waters filled with sulphur and iron. This helped, but the disease continued to plague her.

Early in August, as Sally and Spencer were riding along, she had a strange presentiment of her coming death. Passing a little secluded cemetery at Pleasant Grove, about three miles from the mountain and near to a few houses known as Anderson's Town, she called on her companion to stop. Looking wistfully at the cemetery, she commented on the attractiveness of the quiet and the seclusion of this graveyard. 'Spencer,' she said quietly, 'I have a horror of city burying-places. They do not let even the dead rest, near cities. Promise me, when I am dead, that you will lay me here — here in this quiet place!' There he made a solemn promise to honour her request.

In just a few days after this she went down with typhoid fever. Her husband and son were there to care for her as well as they possibly could. Spencer expressed his wish that she would soon recover and he could take her back to New York. 'I shall go home — to heaven — from this mountain this time, dearest,' she quietly replied. On 15 August it was evident to all that her time of departure had come. Her husband asked her directly if Jesus was with her as she approached the dark valley of death. She looked happily into his eyes and whispered the name of her Saviour. She never spoke again and about ten o'clock she fell asleep in Christ. And so Spencer Cone, who had gently led this once stiff and cultured formalist to a simple faith in Jesus and made her a Baptist, was at her side, holding her hand as she slipped into eternity.

Spencer Cone's wife was the joy of his life. Her constant attention in the family circle, faithful support during his many trials, and sacrificial service for his Lord had sustained and inspired him through the many years of his life. She was also deeply loved by her boys. 'She was all the world to them, the comfort and idol of their lives,' they wrote. But she was no more. When Edward came into the room shortly after she had died, he found his father sitting alone, his head bowed listlessly upon his breast. Seeing him weep, Spencer said softly, 'Weep on, my boy, you are young. Your poor old father has not been able to weep yet.' At that moment 'we felt more bitterly for him who was left desolate, than for her who had gone before'.

The world has never appreciated the mighty role godly women have had in the ministry of the gospel of Jesus Christ. For Baptists who take the Bible as their sole authority and view it as final in matters of faith and practice, women are to assume a private role not a public one, as far as preaching is concerned. But in private and personal ministry, in prayer, in giving, in daily caring for the members of the church, in teaching women and children, and in encouraging and supporting their preacher husbands, their work is vital and their influence is immeasurable. Some men who have never had the benefit of a spiritually-minded companion have nonetheless carried on a powerful work for Christ in the roles of pastors, missionaries and evangelists. But such have been the exception rather than the rule. Here and there we see a David Brainerd, an Asahel Nettleton, or a John Stott with gifts to serve God in the celibate life. But a more general pattern is for God to give to Jonathan Edwards his Sarah and to Charles Spurgeon his Suzannah in order to help the man succeed. 'Who can find a virtuous wife?' asked King Lemuel. 'For her worth is far above rubies. The heart of her husband safely trusts her' (Prov. 31:10-11, NKJV). Spencer Cone was given, by a sovereign God, a wonderful woman to walk with him along the rough and crooked road of life. To her is due a lot of credit for his success.

Of her, Cone said in a letter to Baron Stow, 'My dear Sally was one of the best of wives. True and faithful, industrious and loving, making her house a place of rest and happiness for her husband always, for more than forty-one years, whatever might have been the occasional trials and annoyances without — whatever the toils and anxieties of a pastor's life; and you will believe that *mine* have been not a few. I am left alone, and yet not alone, for Christ is with me; his rod and staff they comfort me.' To his old friend, John L. Dagg, he wrote, 'The Lord has indeed removed from me the desire of my eyes with a stroke! My best earthly friend, the mother of my children, the wife of my youth and of my old age. It was a heavy stroke, but I remembered that the hand which inflicted the blow was the same hand that was nailed to the cross *for me*, *for her*, and I was dumb — I opened not my mouth to complain; I shed no tear; I was a wonder, not only to many; but most — most of all to myself.'[8]

The preacher for Sally Cone's funeral was her husband. In the little chapel at Pleasant Grove, 'with a strange, unnatural power and calmness,' he comforted himself and the people with their hope in Jesus Christ. To all who came, it seemed that his willingness and indeed his God-given ability to perform this last official act over her life was 'an unequalled spectacle of Christian heroism'. Not women only but hardened men of the world, some of whom had come to Schooley's Mountain for amusement, wept like children. One woman who attended the funeral said, 'If I could die as she did, I would pray to die tonight.'

Faithful to his promise Spencer Cone buried his beloved Sally in the little cemetery at Pleasant Grove. There her remains lie, awaiting, with his, the coming of Jesus and the resurrection.

20.

Dying on the field of battle

With the loss of his wife of some forty-two years, the primary earthly support of Spencer Cone was gone. Back in his home on Broome Street in New York as family members and guests passed by his study door in the evening, they saw an old man sitting in his arm chair, with his head thrown listlessly back and 'his whole figure wearing the appearance of weakness and exhaustion'. Here Sally had sat with him through the years sewing or reading a book while he paced the floor backwards and forwards, talking to himself about various subjects and conversing with her about what was on his mind. He was obviously very lonely, and his sons knew that the one whose presence had invigorated him for so long would never be by his side again.

The members of his church never detected any reduction in his energies as a pastor; in fact, he preached with even more power and energy, if possible. He attended faithfully to his preaching, administrative and shepherding duties. But among the people in his intimate circle, there was no doubt that his health was declining. More effort was required for the same level of activity. He said to Edward and Spencer, his sons, 'I am getting old, boys, and feel hard work more than I used to do.'

Thomas Armitage, a young pastor much influenced by Cone and a leading Baptist historian of the period, had an opportunity to see first-hand the inward stress the loss of his wife placed upon Cone. At the time of Sally's death he was pastor of the

Norfolk Street Baptist Church of New York City. A young minister lost his wife and brought her remains to the church on
Norfolk Street where the funeral service was to be held. Cone
was present and was called upon to address the friends of the
deceased. As he arose to speak, with a glance of his eye, he
saw his young brother sitting before the coffin of his sleeping
wife, trembling with emotion. For the sensitive heart of a man
who had just gone through the same experience, it was too
much. For a few moments the great orator, who had braved
the tensions of the pulpit before great crowds everywhere, was
silenced. The words in his mind stuck in his throat so he could
not speak. Then tears began to burst from his eyes and poured
down his cheeks. Finally, with Herculean effort, he regathered
his composure, and said, 'in tones of hallowed tenderness', 'It
is hard to bury a young wife, my dear brother. But when you
have lived with one forty and two years — the wife of your
youth, the mother of your children, the companion of your lonely
hours, the undeviating and always reliable friend of your whole
life — then, indeed, the stroke is heavy.' At Schooley's Mountain, sitting in stolid silence beside the still body of his spouse,
Cone was unable to weep. But seeing a fellow pastor grieving
over his departed spouse, the pastor's heart within him burst
with sympathy and loosened the ducts of his eyes with tears.

In the words of Thomas Armitage who was his friend, com-
patriot in the Bible translation conflict, and preacher at his own
funeral, the death of his wife was 'a stroke from which he never
fully recovered'. Human life is a subtle interaction of mind, body
and spirit. Bodily pain weighs heavily on the soul. Spiritual and
mental suffering drastically affect the body and produces re-
actions which are conveniently dubbed 'psychosomatic'. Often
physical weakness, disease, and even death follows mental
trauma. Sally's death was a laceration in the deepest recesses
of his soul. He drew heavily from the promises of Christ, and
they sustained him in his darkest hours. But even the

consolations of the Word of God did not allay totally the emptiness of his soul. A part of him was gone. Unplugged, as it were, from the primary human support of his old age, Spencer Cone was doomed to fail himself.

On 5 August, just ten days before the first anniversary of the death of his wife, he complained of numbness in his limbs, especially in his left arm. It was a Sunday and he had led a baptismal service earlier in the day. No immediate alarm was felt, for he had had gall bladder attacks before which had come and gone. Such attacks manifested similar symptoms. He was scheduled to preach, in fact, to serve communion in the afternoon. Family members pleaded with him to retire for the evening and ask the deacons to get a supply for the pulpit. He assured them that it would 'wear off'. He fulfilled his responsibilities at the communion table, bringing a message beforehand on the text: 'No man cometh unto the Father but by me.' He commemorated thus with his people the dying love of Jesus Christ for sinners, 'unto whom his prayer for many months had been "even so, Lord Jesus, come quickly!"' It was his last communion service and his last Sunday sermon.

He spoke again on Tuesday evening to the prayer-meeting at the church, and in this engagement he exhibited a limitation which no one had ever observed before. He seemed to have difficulty in concentration, and several times words failed him. At times he lectured in a rambling and disconnected fashion. He soon began to acknowledge that he was losing his strength as a man and a public servant. A friend from Virginia visited him on 9 August, and Cone said to him, 'I have been working very hard and incessantly, from the age of fourteen till now, and now I begin to feel that my work is done.'

On 10 August, after breakfast, the family circle came into his study as was the custom for Bible reading and prayer. Sometimes he would read a chapter from the Scriptures and, at other times, he would ask someone else to do so. In his last days, he almost always called for a reading of 'one of those sweet psalms of David'. He liked to hear the voices of his family reading the book which was so precious to him. He assumed the task of reading on this particular morning and twice he stopped, as if he was unable to see. After reading, his prayer took on a different form. Normally his prayers were primarily intercessory — as he prayed for missionaries, for the prosperity of the cause of Christ, and for America. But on this occasion his prayers were for himself. He seemed, like Jacob, to be wrestling with God at the foot of the ladder which led up to the throne of God. It was as if he were pleading, 'I will not let Thee go except Thou bless me.' Long had he been an undershepherd in the pasture of the Lord and, on this day, he asked God to permit him to pass his charge into the hands of the Good Shepherd himself. He felt that he had been set as a watchman upon the walls of Zion, and he prayed that he might be found free from the blood of all men. This was his last audible prayer. His sons commented in their biography, 'As he knelt, his Lord had said to him: "Servant, they work is done. Son, come up higher."'

Following this time of family devotion he went upstairs to change his attire, with his son in the next room. Hearing his footsteps his son saw him, pallid of countenance, standing near the door, fumbling with his coat. He was trying unsuccessfully to button his waistcoat. The son asked what the matter was and offered to assist. The father said that his hand was very numb and that he was unable to use it. As he was helped to the bed, his limbs stiffened and he said, 'I am very sick.' Obviously he was having a stroke. A deacon from the church came in at that time and together the two undressed him and rubbed his paralyzed limbs and side. As they were doing so, he said to the deacon, 'I have kept on the harness till my work is done. The spirit of man will sustain his infirmity, but a wounded spirit who can bear? *But I have no wounded spirit.* What a blessed thing it is to know that when we leave this world, we are going to a better place.' Spencer Cone had said on numerous occasions that, like a faithful horse, he wanted to die in the harness. Using a different figure, somewhat more apropos to his personality, he said in a letter to J. L. Dagg, 'I mean, in spite of earth or hell, to die on the field of battle.'[1] This resolve was fulfilled for it had been less than a week since he had preached the gospel. To his credit it can be said that, in the very last days of his life, he never deserted the pulpit for a single Sunday when he had the physical and mental power to preach. After all, the pulpit was his field in the battle for truth, and his love for that platform never left him.

His personal physicians were called in and, with all the kindness and the medical skills available, they tried to bring him back to his normal condition. But Cone had had a severe stroke and he drifted slowly into a state of complete paralysis. The body which had served him so well, the magnificent mind, and the voice that had heralded forth the sovereign grace of God, were useless for any practical purpose. The doctors told the family that even if he recovered, he would never preach again. With that final word they were at peace, for they knew his desire was to live only as he was able to proclaim the gospel. 'And so,' said Edward, 'the hand that struck him down at once, upon the battle field, was full of mercy.' For him death was better than inactivity.

On Tuesday morning, 28 August 1855, after living seventy years, three months and twenty-nine days, Spencer Cone left the scene of his earthly pilgrimage and service and went home to be with his Lord. It was the day for the weekly lecture of the pastor, but no lecture was given. Instead Dr T. T. Devan, a beloved friend and his personal physician, led the church in a time of praise and prayer: praise that God had given them such a faithful pastor for fourteen years and prayer that God, in his goodness, would enable the church to experience continued blessings in the future. 'All felt that their father was gone; and they sorrowed, because he was not there to lead the service, but most of all, because they should see his face no more.'[2] That afternoon at one o'clock many members of the church, the Board of Managers and Life directors of the American Bible Union assembled to plan appropriate resolutions and memorial services. The meeting was chaired by Wm. H. Wyckoff, Esq., Cone's associate in Bible translation. Rev. C. J. Hopkins, pastor of the Bethesda Baptist Church, daughter church of First Baptist, led in prayer as all 'bowed the knee before the throne of grace'. Following the meeting those present walked in procession to the Cone residence, where many ministers of various denominations had gathered to express their high regard for the deceased. Following prayer by B. M. Hill, Corresponding Secretary of the American Baptist Home Mission Society, a solemn procession formed and slowly walked, following the corpse, to the meeting house. The pall bearers were members of the church who had sat under Cone's ministry. William Colgate would have been a pall bearer, but he was out of town.

A memorial service was held, conducted by Dr T. T. Devan. The meeting house was crowded, and thousands were turned away. Officials at the service included Rev. E. L. Magoon, pastor of Oliver Street Baptist Church, where Spencer Cone had laboured for eighteen years, Dr I. Ferris, President of New York University, and A. D. Gillette, pastor of the Calvary Baptist Church, later to become famous as editor of the printed minutes from 1707 to 1807 of the Philadelphia Baptist Association. Rev. S. H. Cox also made a few remarks, referring to his early acquaintance with the deceased and his love for him as a faithful man of God. The audience then slowly departed from the building, passing in front of the coffin, to view, for the last time, the features of their beloved friend, brother and pastor.

On Friday, 31 August, the remains of Cone were borne by the family, accompanied by a few friends, to Schooley's Mountain, where he was laid to rest beside his late wife, Sally. Wyckoff

Tombstone of Sally Cone

Pine Grove Presbyterian Church, Schooley's Mountain, where Spencer and Sally Cone are buried

made a few remarks and Rev. C. A. Buckbee pronounced the benediction. The remaining members of the family and the few friends there retired then to their homes, 'feeling that they had given back to earth one of the best and noblest of God's gifts to man'.

A funeral sermon, later printed at the request of the church, was delivered by Rev. Thomas Armitage on Sunday, 16 September at 3:00 p.m. As was the case at the original service of memorial, thousands were turned away from the meeting house which was much too small to hold the crowds. The text of Thomas Armitage was Job 5:26: 'Thou shalt come to the grave, in hoary age, as the sheaf is gathered in, in its season,' appropriately a translation of the *Revised Version* of the American Bible Union. The sermon, obviously carefully composed, runs to some fifty-one pages, and is an excellent sample of nineteenth century pulpit eloquence. With florid language and in classical style, almost artificial in its lofty rhetorical exuberance, the personal merits of the subject are extolled. Reference is made to his achievements and appropriate comments are made on his theological convictions. Armitage obviously wanted to make his mark by this funeral oration, and it is safe to say he succeeded in his attempt.

And so in August 1855, ended the life, along with its final memorials and tributes, of a remarkable man of God. In this same year, far away from New York City across the broad Atlantic, a young minister, who had also followed a succession of eminent Baptist preachers in his own pulpit, had begun to publish his sermons, which were attracting much attention throughout the City of London. The first sentence in the preface to his printed sermons is 'The preaching of the Word by the chosen servants of the Living God, is the ordained means of the gathering in of the elect. It is not the Word of God *read*, so much as that which is *heard,* which has the promise attached to it; hence the importance of a devout attendance on the ministry of the gospel.'[3] The similarities between Spencer Houghton Cone and Charles Haddon Spurgeon cannot escape the notice of anyone familiar with these two giants of the pulpit. But more will be said about this similarity in the next chapter.

21.

The legacy of

Spencer Houghton Cone

Many would argue that the world should be content to leave the life of the man which we have just chronicled hidden safely in the archives of the few Baptist institutions which have intentionally, or perhaps accidentally, preserved it. The remains of Spencer and Sally Cone rest peacefully in the little cemetery in Schooley's Mountain, New Jersey, and till now little attention has been given to their ministry. But their boys loved them and believed that posterity should not forget; and so they gathered materials from their own family records, from the testimonies of mutual friends, and, of course, from their own memories and put together a book which records their own devotion and respect. Obviously this writer agrees with the sons of Cone that the witness of these lives should be passed on to posterity. Indeed, as I hope to show, thousands, perhaps millions, are still today benefiting from their sacrificial labours. There are a number of blessings Baptists enjoy today which Spencer Cone in *some measure* helped to provide, along with his beloved wife, without whose faithful assistance it could not have been accomplished.

Freedom

People living in the free world, and this includes the United Kingdom, the United States, Canada, Australia, continental

Europe, and thankfully today we can say to a great extent even Eastern Europe, have a tendency to take their privileges for granted. That is especially true of the younger generation in the first mentioned countries who have experienced no major war in their lifetime. They can travel about as they wish, go to church or stay at home according to their preferences, and go to the ballot box and vote. They have free access to many different translations of the Bible and, in many cases, if they desire they can turn on the radio or TV and hear a message from the Bible. How did such privileges come about?

They came about because many men and women of past generations had enough concern for their families and communities to devote time and energy to their preservation, and because they were willing to risk even their lives to stand bravely against political tyranny and oppression. The idea that people have the inherent right to speak, write and worship according to the dictates of their conscience is a relatively new idea. It was spawned for the most part in Britain, tested in parts of Europe, and then finally truly implemented in the United States of America. But not without a terrible price. Several major wars have been fought to secure the rights of man with which human beings have been 'endowed by their Creator', as Thomas Jefferson said in the Declaration of Independence. The twentieth century saw several attempts by powerful leaders of personal ambition and expansionist design to crush political and religious freedom. But till now the nations which have, to a great extent, known the impact of the gospel of Jesus Christ have stood shoulder to shoulder to resist and to defeat successfully such designs.

Spencer and Sally Cone, and indeed the whole historic family tradition of which they were a part, were early advocates of these freedoms. For them 'the voluntary principle', which now seems to be taken for granted in Britain and America, was sacrosanct. They were willing not only to advocate this principle with all the vigour of their minds, but also they were willing to fight for it. Spencer hesitated not to enlist in the military service of his country when the need arose. Indeed, even as 'The Star Spangled Banner' was being written in Baltimore harbour, he was bravely standing on the shore, in the line of fire, defending his country. Today that flag, and indeed the Union Jack as well, stands for freedom to work and worship, freedom to speak and write, freedom to educate our children and manage the earth God gave us. If we believe that patriotism is compatible with the Christian faith, indeed, if we believe that one should be willing to give the full measure of devotion, even life itself, for one's country, then Spencer Cone is a model. He is one of many who have stood in the breach for freedom.

Bible translations

As the year 2000 approached an international panel of 400 scholars gathered to draw up a list of the 100 most influential people of the past millennium. This list was not about the *best* people or the most *moral* people, but the most influential — those who had made the most lasting impact on the world and civilization. This was a group of scholars from many different disciplines, political and philosophical ideologies. What a daunting task they had. Names such as Albert Einstein, Christopher Columbus, William Shakespeare and Charles Darwin ranked high on the list. But the three chosen as being the most important in changing the course of history were, to this writer at least, somewhat surprising. The third most influential was Sir Isaac Newton, the amazing mathematician and natural philosopher who by his investigations and experiments laid the foundations for modern science. The second most influential was the German preacher, Martin Luther, who challenged medieval bondage by rediscovering the great truth that a man can obtain peace with

God through a personal act of faith without the intervening mediation of the church. But the most influential of all was the German printer, Johann Gutenberg, who invented moveable type. By his efforts ordinary people, who had formerly relied on the spoken word for information, could gain access to the great written works of man. And what was the first book he printed? The German Bible.

Throughout the history of the English-speaking world there have been many who have striven to make available for us the Word of God in our native tongue. Chief among these, of course, were John Wyckliffe and William Tyndale. These men of scholarship translated the Scriptures and were instrumental in distributing it to the masses. Tyndale died as a martyr for his trouble.

Many hundreds of other lesser-known figures, too numerous to mention, have also laboured to secure for us the best manuscripts of the original text of Holy Scripture. Others have striven to provide improved translations more easily read and understood in contemporary language. Spencer Cone took a great interest in this cause. He was a leader in early Bible societies in the United States and personally gave of his time and substance to distribute the Scriptures not only at home but also on the mission field. 'The Lord gave the word,' said King David. 'Great was the company of those that published it' (Ps. 68:11). Count Spencer Cone in that great company of publishers and proclaimers of the Bible.

Cone's altercations with many of his brethren about the need to *translate* and not just *transfer* the meaning of 'baptizo' were, perhaps, regrettable. Even his dear friend and partner in ministry, J. L. Dagg, disagreed with his stance on this issue. But after all it was not lack of zeal, dedication and conviction that embroiled him in this controversy. Some would argue that he was actually right, perhaps ahead of his times. But be that as it may, he knew the importance of correct Bible translations, and he was willing even to amend the beloved *Authorized Version* itself, if necessary, for people to know properly the true meaning of Scripture. It was because of the efforts of men like Cone that the world has seen the English and American revised versions, as well as many that have come since. Cone could see the defects in the *Authorized Version* and was honest and courageous enough to speak out about them.

A testimony

The sons of Spencer Cone left behind a beautiful account of how a man overcame great personal hardships and disappointments to succeed in life. The struggles he faced, the obstacles he overcame, the sufferings he sustained to survive in this world certainly should be a source of inspiration to everyone.

What a marvellous example the loving relationship between Spencer and Sally Cone has left for us all to follow. In a day when nearly half of all marriages fail, and when even in evangelical circles divorce is rampant, the beautiful union of these two people shows the wonderful results of human love, experienced and practised as God intended. Their well-attested devotion to each other and the God who saved them is worthy of emulation by Christian young people everywhere. What power there is in the *united* service of a man and woman who have dedicated their lives to promoting the gospel.

But aside from the fascinating personal victories of Spencer Cone and the tender marriage union which he enjoyed, his experience of divine grace is a reminder of the power of the gospel itself. He was converted primarily through reading the testimony of the English preacher, John Newton, whose own career is a marvellous witness to the grace of God. Pre-eminently John, and even Spencer also, learned through the powerful operations of the Holy Spirit what it is first to recognize one's sinful condition and then to experience deliverance through faith

in the atoning sacrifice of Jesus Christ. Paul the apostle, formerly a self-righteous Pharisee, an enemy of the gospel and a
persecutor of God's people, was ready at any time to share
what happened to him on the road to Damascus. He wanted
the world to know what God had done for him, even as he
wrote inspired Scripture. We also have the authentic account of
how an erstwhile educator, actor, and newspaper editor who
was proud, ambitious and self-sufficient came to bow the knee
before the cross of Jesus Christ. There is a great cloud of witnesses on record, telling us how the multitudes hung on Cone's
words as he mounted the sacred desk to proclaim the good
news to perishing sinners. This is quite a story.

The church

As has already been mentioned Spencer Cone left behind no
books or printed volumes of sermons. What a loss that is. But
he was supremely committed to establishing a great church,
and in this he was successful. He loved the local church, and
for it he gave the full devotion of his mind and body. The institution which he did so much to nurture, the First Baptist Church
of New York City, known to succeeding generations as the
'Mother Church of New York Baptists', has gone through many
changes since 1855 when it paid its last respects to its beloved
pastor. But the diligent labours of the likes of John Gano and
Spencer Cone continued to bear fruit for many generations,
and indeed, if this writer is to be any judge, still continue to do
so even to the present. The church has continued to adhere to
the fundamental teachings of the Baptist faith, though not always
evidently in the Calvinistic direction characteristic of Cone's
ministry. Succeeding him was Kingdom Nott, who was tragic-
ally drowned after only twenty-two months in his post. Twelve
men have since occupied this position. Without a doubt the

most famous, and perhaps the most gifted, was I. M. Haldeman who was a leader in the fundamentalist movement which resisted modernism at the turn of the century. He was pastor of First Baptist for forty-nine years, removed from office only by his death in 1933.

During the pastorate of Thomas Anderson (1862-1878) in 1882 the church moved from the Broome and Elisabeth Streets location to a new gothic-styled building at the corner of 39th Street and Park Avenue. Haldeman's preaching attracted such crowds that another new building, the one now in use, was constructed at the corner of 79th Street and Broadway in 1891. This magnificent structure, which after the addition of a balcony in 1903 seats about a thousand people, has been described as having an 'inexplicable iconography'. The architect, George M. Keister, applied a biblically related symbolism to the building. The taller tower had at its top an electric light and is understood to represent Christ, the head of the church and the light of the world. The lower tower, which appears to be incomplete, was designed to represent the church which will remain incomplete until the return of Christ. The two towers, one cylindrical and one octagonal, appear to be Romanesque in design, while other parts of the building leave a decidedly Early Christian/Byzantine flavour.

Inside the church is a large hall with a number of original portraits, including one of I. M. Haldeman and a three-quarter length painting of Spencer Cone as a young man, standing in a posture of preaching with his right hand raised (see page 143). In a smaller room are fascinating facsimiles of two original paintings, now at William Jewell College in Kansas City, representing the colonial patriot and pastor, John Gano. In one he is seen baptizing George Washington (see page 104) and in the other he is seen as a chaplain praying for the American troops during the revolutionary war. Many of the records of the ministry of Spencer Cone are housed there, including a book listing all the marriages he solemnized (see page 91).

More important than the architecture or archival resources of this church, is its continual evangelical witness in New York City. Nominally affiliated with the General Association of Regular Baptist Churches, the church has not swerved from its adherence to the authority of Scripture. After some years of decline a group of young professionals is now moving into the church and helping to bring about a time of renewal. According to the present minister, Rev. Robert Gage, who gave this writer a courteous tour of the building and showed him the records of interest, the congregation consists of some two hundred people, which, considering the difficulties of inner-city ministry, is respectable. The congregation travels, for the most part, to the church by subway or bus, since there is no church parking area.

International missionary enterprise

In the history of Christianity we can see how God, after the death of the original apostles, has raised up leaders and movements to propagate the true faith of the New Testament Church. In the early ages of the church, through great leaders such as Athanasius and through various councils, the orthodox doctrine of the Trinity was defined. The African Bishop, Augustine, wrote in defence of the teachings of Jesus and Paul on subjects such as sin and grace. The Reformers recovered the fundamental truth of the finality and sufficiency of Scripture and the blessed doctrine of justification by faith. The Puritans investigated and expounded the essential meaning of sanctification and wrote extensively on the relation of law and grace.

It was not, however, until the times of the Great Awakenings in England and America that the church really began to take seriously Jesus's command to take the gospel to the whole world. In the late eighteenth and nineteenth centuries the evangelical church was stirred up to make evangelization and international

Interior views of First Baptist Church sanctuary

missions a priority. The primary leaders of this movement are well known to us: Eliot, Brainerd, Carey, Burns, Hudson Taylor, Judson, and a host of others. Since their pioneer labours, all the branches of the churches which sprang from the awakenings — Presbyterian, Methodist and Baptist, as well as others — have devoted much time, financial resources and organization to send the gospel out into the whole world. Southern Baptists alone now have over 5,000 missionaries in over 100 countries proclaiming the good news of the gospel. Various translation societies have sent thousands of scholars to foreign fields to translate the Word of God into all languages and dialects.

Any fair examination of the facts should be able to illustrate and acknowledge the primary role of Spencer Cone in these early missionary efforts. In the first half of the nineteenth century, he was considered by his Baptist brethren to be the most influential advocate of missions among them. He held a position of leadership in the first organized cooperative effort of Baptists to send out heralds to the nations. His church sponsored conferences under his leadership and housed agencies in the New York area which coordinated missionary work. He personally prayed, wrote, gave and promoted to advance the spreading of the gospel. Truly Spencer Cone was one of the architects who laid the foundations of modern missionary organizations. Finally, and perhaps most importantly, he was a personal friend of every true missionary. Missionaries ate at his table, slept in his home and shared the warmth of his family circle. There has never lived a greater friend to missionaries than Spencer Cone.

Cone and Spurgeon

Previously it was noted that there are some similarities between the subject of this book and the English preacher, Charles

Spurgeon. The differences are obvious. Spurgeon's historical impact has been incomparably greater because he left behind such a wealth of literature; in fact, this author is of the understanding that there are more titles in print by this man than by any other individual living or dead. For that reason alone Spurgeon remains in a class of his own. But Cone and Spurgeon were alike in many ways. Both believed, loved and preached the system of theology known as the 'doctrines of grace'.[1] Both laboured, Cone in New York and Spurgeon in London, in the greatest cities of the Western world. Because of the sheer strategic geographical location of their churches they wielded immense influence. Both were supremely gifted as preachers of the gospel, having capacious minds, powerful voices and exceptional ability to communicate the Word of God in everyday language, understood by ordinary people. Both were tender-hearted and loving in pastoral relations, though unbending and relentless in their stand for the truth. Both were assisted by wives of remarkable intelligence, culture and dedication to their ministries. And, we might add as a final touch, both had two sons who adored them and followed in their footsteps of faith.

In the books of the Bible the faithful labours of those who heralded God's truth are recorded. Their trials and triumphs, their foibles and failures are faithfully written. With this precedent before us, it is our duty first to discover and then, as opportunity affords, to relate to our own generation what God has wrought through those who have served the same God since the book of Divine revelation was closed. With this apologia, we conclude this delightful journey into the life and testimony of God's servant, Spencer Houghton Cone: teacher, soldier, editor, chaplain, husband, father, pastor, missionary entrepreneur and correspondent, who was a friend to every good cause and an enemy of all in opposition to it. Like the saints blessed by the voice from heaven in the apocalypse, he 'died in the Lord'; and we doubt not that Spencer and Sally

Cone can be embraced in the response of the Holy Spirit, that they 'rest from their labours, and their works follow them'.

Appendix I
The First Baptist Church

The First Baptist Church, in the City of New York, was founded in the year 1745. The members met together in private dwellings until 1753, when they hired a Sail Loft in Cart and Horse Street, now William Street, where they statedly assembled for public worship for several years. As their numbers and resources increased, they purchased ground in Gold Street, and built upon it a small Meeting House, which was opened on the 14th of March, 1760. This house was removed, and a large stone building was erected upon the same site in 1802. In the present year, 1841, this building was also taken down, and a large and commodious edifice for the use of the Church, together with offices for Bible and Missionary operations connected with the Baptist denomination, has been erected at the corner of Broome and Elizabeth Streets; a representation of which may be seen on the cover.

The doctrines in the belief and profession of which this church was constituted, and which she still steadfastly maintains, are contained in our first book of Records, pages 3 — 6: but as our predecessors authenticate their views only by a reference to the Scriptures as a whole, we deem it expedient and proper to publish the Summary of our Faith, and Articles of our CHURCH COVENANT; referring to particular passages in proof of our peculiar tenets.

Appendix II

A Summary of the Faith and Practice, with the Articles of the Covenant of The First Baptist Church in the City of New York Spencer H. Cone, pastor

The following Summary of Faith and Practice, with the Articles of the Church Covenant, were unanimously adopted, in their present form, at a regular Church Meeting, July 28th, 1841.

Spencer Houghton Cone
Pastor
S. Pier, Church Clerk

Summary of Faith and Practice

1. We receive the Holy Scriptures of the Old and New Testaments as being ALL GIVEN BY INSPIRATION OF GOD; and as containing the only authorized RULE of our faith and practice. 2 Tim. iii. 16. 2 Pet. i. 21. Isa. xxxiv. John v. 39. Acts xvii. 11. 1 Pet. iv. 11. Isa. viii. 20. Ps. Cxix. 105. Prov. Xiii. 13. John viii. 31.

2. According to these Holy Oracles, we believe that there is ONE, and but ONE LIVING AND TRUE GOD, who subsisteth in THREE EQUAL PERSONS, the FATHER, the SON, and the HOLY SPIRIT.

Deut. vi. 4. Mark xii. 29. Eph. iv. 6. 1 Tim. ii. 5. Exod. xx. 3—5. Gen. i. 26. Isa xlvii. 16. Matt. xxviii. 19. 1 John v. 7. 2 Cor. xiii. 14. Heb. i. 3. Isa. ix. 6. John i.1. Isa. xlvi. 9. John x. 30.

3. That God is clearly revealed, as to his being and perfections, both by His works and in His Word; yet, that with respect to his Essence, mode of Existence, and manner of operation, He is incomprehensible to all but himself.
Rom. i. 20. Ps. xix. 1—3. Job xi. 7—9. Isa. xl. 28. Isa. xlv. 15.

4. That God alone created the Heavens and the Earth, with all their inhabitants and appurtenances, whether visible or invisible.
Ps. xxxiii. 6—9. Gen. i. 1. Acts xvii. 24—26. Gen. ii. 1. Ps. viii. 3. Ps. civ. 24. John i. 3. Col. i. 16.

5. That God made man upright, and able to keep the Law under which He placed him; but that man, being left to the freedom of his own will, transgressed that Law, and thereby fell into a state of moral depravity and legal condemnation.
Gen. i. 26. Eccl. vii. 29. Gen. i. 31. Ps. viii. 5. Gen. v. 1. Gen. iii. 7. Isa. i. 5. Ps. xiv. 3. John iii. 18. Rom. v. 12. 18. Isa. xliii. 27. Rom. i. 28—32.

6. That the first man, Adam, was constituted, by divine appointment, a public head and representative of all his posterity; and consequently when he fell, they all fell with him into the same condition.
Rom. v. 14. 12. 19. 1 Cor. xv. 22, 48, 49. Gen. v. 3. Job xiv. 4.

7. That all mankind, by nature, are totally and universally depraved, and therefore without either ability or inclination to return to God, or to render perfect obedience to his moral requirements.

# # #

: Appendix II: Confession of the First Baptist Church

Appendix II: Confession of the First Baptist Church 197

Ps. liii. 3. Rom. iii. 9—20. Prov. xx. 9. Josh. xxiv.19. Jer. xiii. 23. John v. 40. Jer. ii. 22. John vi. 44. 65. Eph. ii, 3.

8. That notwithstanding these deplorable facts, whereas Adam, by his own personal transgression, lost his ability to keep the Law under which he was made; and whereas the disability, as well as the disinclination of his posterity to keep this Law, arises from their personal depravity; it evidently follows, that their obligations to render a perfect obedience to all God's commandments, remain undiminished; and consequently that the penal curse threatened against every delinquent is strictly righteous.
Gen. iii. 16, 17. Job xxi. 14. Gen. vi. 5. Deut. vi. 5. Luke x. 25 —28. Gal. iii. 10. James ii. 10. Rom. ii. 2—15.

9. We believe in the indispensable necessity of the ATONE- MENT OF CHRIST, and its special relationship to the sins of his people.
Luke xxiv. 26. Rom. viii. 3. Isa. liii. 10, 11. Lev. xvi. 30. Heb. ix. 22. Matt. i. 21. John x. 11. Heb. x. 10. 1 Pet. i. 18, 19. Luke i. 68. Rev. v. 9. Eph. i. 7. Rev. xiv. 4. Tit. ii. 14. Rev. vii. 14—17. Isa. Ii. 11. 1 Cor. i. 30. Gal. i. 4. 1 Cor. xv. 3.

10. That God, in pardoning and justifying any of the fallen race of mankind, has no respect to any supposed good works to be done by them, either before or after regeneration; but alone to the obedience and sacrifice of Christ, which God the Father, by an act of his mere grace, imputes to all that believe, as the only meritorious cause of their pardon and justification.
Ez. xxxvi. 31. 32. Luke xvii. 10. Rom. iii. 9—28. iv. 4—8 16, 23—25. Eph. ii. 1—10. Isa. xliii. 25. Jer. xxxiii. 6. Rom. iii. 21—28. iv. 3—6. 23—25. v.19—21. Acts, xiii. 39. xviii. 27.

11. That no works performed by any, prior to their regeneration and faith in Christ, are spiritually good; yet morality and

benevolence are to be enjoined on all, as required by the Law of God, and as useful in society; and that believers especially are to be careful to maintain good works, as the fruits and evidences of their gracious state; as the means of their usefulness in the church and in the world; and by which they show forth the praises of Him who hath called them out of darkness into his marvellous light.

Rom. viii. 7, 8. Heb. xi. 6. Isa. i 16, 17. Ez. ii. 3—5. Luke x. 27. Eph. ii. 10. Titus ii. 11—14. iii. 8. Philemon 5—7. Matt. vii. 16. Gal. vi. 10. Heb. xiii. 16. 1 Pet. ii. 9. Matt. v. 16.

12. That the Gospel of the grace of God, revealing his method of saving lost sinners, through the incarnation, obedience, and death of Christ, is to be preached to mankind in common; but that regeneration, and therefore repentance toward God and faith toward our Lord Jesus Christ, which are essential not only to salvation but to the enjoyment of peace with God, and to the performance of his acceptable service; as also every requisite to secure perseverance in grace to glory, (which is certain of all the regenerate;)—are sovereignly bestowed according to God's eternal and personal election of his people in Christ, through whom He gives his Holy Spirit to them, for their effectual calling, sanctification, and preservation unto eternal life.

Acts xx. 24. 2 Tim. i. 10. 2 Cor. iv. 6. Gen,. iii. 15. Isa. vii. 14. Matt. i. 21. v. 17. 1 Pet. iii. 18. Matt. xxviii. 19. Mark xvi. 15. Luke xxiv. 47. Col. i. 28. Acts xxi. 21. xxvi. 18. Rom. v. 1. Heb. xi. 6. Rom. viii. 8. 17. 30. John x. 27—29. Acts xiii. 48. Eph. i. 3, 4. 1 Thes. v. 9. 2 Tim. i. 9. Tit. iii. 5—7. Eph. iv. 30. Rom. viii. 11.

13. That although the Holy Spirit as to his testimony in the Scriptures and in the ministry of the word, is constantly resisted by the unregenerate, as He was by the Jews as to his testimony

by the prophets and apostles; yet, that in his regenerating operations He is always invincible and infallible.
Acts vii. 51. Neh. ix. 30. Zech. vii. 11. Eph. ii. 1, 4, 5. Philip. i. 6. Rom. viii. 14. 2 Cor. iii. 17.

14. Moreover, in regard to the future state, we believe that according to the Scriptures there will be a personal resurrection both of the just and unjust; and that besides an individual judgment that passes upon every soul on its separation from the body, there will be a general judgment, when an eternal separation will be made between the righteous and the wicked;—the righteous being received to everlasting happiness, and the wicked being consigned to everlasting misery.
Dan. xii. 1—3. John v. 28, 29. Acts xxiv. 15. Luke xvi. 22, 23. xxiii. 43. Heb. ix. 27. Acts xvii. 81. Rom. xiv. 10. 2 Cor. v. 10. Rev. xx. 11—15. Matt. xxv. 31—46. 2 Thess. i. 6—10. 1 Cor. xv. 4, 16, 20, 49. Luke xxiii. 43.

15. Nor would we presume to form our views of the church and ordinances of Christ by any other light than that of the same inspired oracles: and judging by these infallible records, we believe that the kingdom of Christ is not of this world; that the gospel church, therefore, is neither national nor parochial, and that none belong to her by virtue of their natural descent from her members. A visible Gospel Church should consist of such persons only as make a credible profession of faith in Christ, receive his gospel and obey his precepts.
John xviii. 36. Isa liv. 5. 13. Eph. v. 32. Isa. lix. 21. Acts ii. 47. 1 Cor. i. 1, 2. Col. i. 2. Col. iv. 15. Acts ix. 31.

16. We believe that every gospel church, regularly constituted, is a society independent of every other ecclesiastical body; having a scriptural authority and directory to govern itself; to choose and remove its own officers, and to discipline its own members.

Matt. xviii. 15—17. Rom. xiv. 1. 1 Cor. v. 11—13. Acts vi.
3—5. 1 John iv. 1. Acts xiv. 23.

17. That the only Officers belonging to organized gospel
churches, are Bishops and Deacons.
Philip. i. 1. 1 Tim. iii. 1—13. Acts xiv. 23. xx. 17. 28.

18. That the only symbolic ordinances appertaining to the gospel
dispensation, are Baptism and the Lord's Supper: that nothing
is a scriptural administration of baptism, but a total immersion
of the subject in water, in the Name of the Holy Trinity, by a
man duly authorized to administer gospel ordinances. We also
believe that subjection to baptism is prerequisite to admission
into a visible church, and therefore, to partaking of the Lord's
Supper; which is to be received only by members of a visible
church, and by them only when come together in a church
capacity.
Matt. xxviii. 19, 20. Acts ii. 41, 42. Matt. xxvi. 26—28. 1 Cor.
xi. 33, 34. Acts xx. 7.

19. We believe that the first day of the week is emphatically the
LORD'S DAY; and that it becometh us, laying aside ordinary
labour and recreation, to hail every return of this day with
christian gladness, and to spend the hours of it in such devo-
tional exercises, private, domestic, and public, as God may
afford us opportunity and ability to perform; excepting only
such works of necessity and mercy as the events of Providence
may dictate or require.
Heb. iv. 3. 9. Col. ii. 16, 17. John xx. 19—26. Rev. i.10. Acts
xx. 7. 1 Cor. xvi, 2.

20. We believe, moreover, that the singing of psalms, hymns,
and Spiritual songs, is divinely enjoined, and when religiously
performed is well pleasing to God. And though we are assured

that none but the regenerate sing with the spirit and with the understanding, we nevertheless believe that mankind in common, as they are constantly receiving various mercies and blessings from God, are bound to celebrate his praise; and, therefore, that they should be allowed and encouraged to join in this part of public worship.

Eph. v. 19. Col. iii. 16. Heb. xiii. 15, 16. 1 Cor. xiv. 15. Ps. xxxiv. 1, 2. Ps. cvii. 8. 21. 31. Acts xvii. 24—29, Rom. i. 20, 21. Ps. cxlv. 4. 10.

Church Covenant

ART. I. We agree to and adopt the preceding Summary, as a Compendium of our Faith and Practice; believing it to be in accordance with the doctrines and precepts of the Holy Scriptures.

ART. II. Besides observing private and family worship, We agree "Not to forsake the assembling of ourselves together" for public worship, on the Lord's day, and at such other seasons, whether stated or occasional, as the church, from time to time, shall appoint for this purpose. Psalm lxxxvii. 2. Heb. x. 25.

ART. III. Believing it to be our duty, as a church of Christ, to maintain the order and discipline which He hath appointed in His house, We agree to hold such meetings, stated and occasional, for transacting church-business, as our circumstances may require; and that, having appointed such meetings, we will be careful, Providence permitting, to attend them.

ART. IV. To preserve and promote peace and concord among us, with purity of faith and practice, We agree that it is our duty to pursue and support the following measures :—1. That in cases of private or personal grievance, the member aggrieved, should observe the injunctions of our blessed Lord: If thy brother shall trespass against thee, go and tell him his fault between thee and him alone, &c. &c. Matt. xviii. 15—17. 2. That any member clearly proved before the church, to have been guilty of gross immorality, should, without further proceeding, be put away. I Cor. v. 11— 13. 3. That any member, habitually neglecting the worship or communion of the church, should be called upon as a delinquent, that it may be known whether such person is an object of Christian sympathy, or of church-censure. Rom. xv. I.—6. Gal. v. 1—12. 4. That any member known to have departed from "the faith of the gospel," as held by the church—or, to have frequented any place of licentious amusement, such as a theatre, a ball-room, or the like, should he rebuked and admonished; and, if found perseveringly impenitent and incorrigible, such person should be put away, as evidently regardless of the peace and reputation of the church, and as a lover of erroneous doctrines and of sensual pleasures, and therefore, not a lover of God. Rom. xii. 1, 2. 1 Cor. xi. 19. .Eph. v. 11. 2 Tim. iii. 4, 5. Heb. x. 23.   5. That members becoming disaffected toward each other touching "things pertaining to this life," such as property or character, shall not be suffered to go to law before any worldly tribunal; but shall be required mutually to submit their matters of controversy to the investigation and judgment of the church; and, therefore, that any member or members refusing to comply with this apostolic direction, shall be censured by the church, and, persisting therein, shall, after due forbearance and labour, be put away. 1 Cor. vi. 1—10. 6. That persons put away, for whatever offence, great or small, on giving to the church satisfactory evidence of repentance and reformation, shall be cordially restored to membership. 2 Cor. ii. 6—11. Gal. vi. 1. Restoration to membership, however, does not include the restoration of a brother to any office that he may have held in the church before his exclusion. For, as no one is promoted to office by his original admission to membership, so, not by his re-admission after having been excluded. Men are to be chosen to office in the church from among its members. Out of the number of his disciples, Christ set apart the twelve and the seventy. Mark iii. 13, 14. Luke x. 1. and out of the churches, elders and deacons were chosen. Acts xiv. 23. chap. vi. 3. and 1 Tim. iii. 8—13.

ART. V. As unanimity in church-acts is always desirable, We agree to use all scriptural means to promote it—such as due forbearance, meek expostulation, and affectionate persuasion; yet, when these fail of conciliating a minority, We agree, that ultimately all questions regularly brought before us, shall be decided by a majority of the members present.

ART. VI. Finding no specified manner of receiving baptized persons into a visible church, either enjoined or exemplified in the New Testament, we believe that every particular church is at liberty to receive such persons in any decent and solemn manner which the church may prefer; they having previously gained fellowship with them, by hearing a relation of their experience, and being credibly assured of their good moral character. Persons presenting LETTERS OF DISMISSION from sister churches of the same faith and order, may be received either on the authority of such letters, or may be required to relate their experience, with an account of their doctrinal views, as the church, in each case, shall judge prudent and expedient: and members of this church, in good standing, may be DISMISSED, at their own request, to unite with any other church of the same faith and order.

ART. VII. In our deportment toward each other—toward the members of sister churches—and toward the community at large, both civil and religious, We agree that we will endeavour, through grace, to maintain "a conversation becoming the gospel of Christ," that in all things, God may be glorified in us, and that his cause upon earth may be promoted through our instrumentality. Philip. i. 27. 1 Pet. iii. and iv. chapters.

ART. VIII. In supporting the gospel and aiding the poor among us—as also in defraying all other expenses necessarily arising from our organization as a church, We agree conscientiously to bear our several proportions, according to our circumstances; that some may not be eased and others burdened; 2 (Cor. viii. 13 :—and inasmuch as the Lord Jesus commanded his disciples to preach the gospel to every creature, we acknowledge it to be our duty and privilege to pray fervently, to labour zealously, and to give cheerfully for the dissemination of divine truth throughout the earth. Isa. lx. 1. Matt. x. 7, 8. Mark xvi. 15.

ART. IX. We agree that it is expedient that all persons who may hereafter propose to unite with us, should give their assent to this Summary of Faith and Practice, and the Articles of this Church Covenant, before their admission. And,

Finally: Sensible of our weakness and liability to err, and, therefore, of our continual dependence on the grace and guidance of the Holy Spirit, We agree, that it becometh us, with much prayer and self-denial, to walk together in all humility and brotherly kindness—to watch over each other for good and not for evil—to stir up one another to love and to good works; and, when circumstances require it, to warn and rebuke, to admonish and exhort one another, according to the rules and precepts of the gospel; all which, may God, for Christ's sake, enable us to do, to the praise of the glory of his grace. Amen.

Appendix III
Principles and Intentions of the American Bible Union

The AMERICAN BIBLE UNION was organized June 10th, 1850, "to procure and circulate the most faithful versions of the Sacred Scriptures in all languages throughout the world."—Constitution.

The Board adopted the following resolution, which was subsequently sanctioned by the Union.

"That appropriations made by the Union, shall in no case be employed for the circulation of a version Which is not made on the following principles, viz: The exact meaning of the inspired text, as that text expressed it to those who understood the original Scriptures at the time they were first written, must be translated by corresponding words and phrases, so far as they can be found, in the vernacular tongue of those for whom the version is designed, with the least possible obscurity or indefiniteness."

In accordance with the object set forth in the Constitution, the Bible Union seeks to procure a faithfully revised version of the English Scriptures and similar versions in other European and in heathen languages. The design is to have the Bible speak with one voice throughout the World.

Missionaries now complain that, as intelligent heathen learn the English language, they discover the palpable discrepancies between our version and the translations made by the missionaries; and they naturally conclude that the latter are wrong, as it is inconceivable that Christians in America should circulate among their own countrymen known errors, and print the truth only to the heathen!

In the version commonly used in this country are many acknowledged errors and obscurities, some affecting the essential doctrines of the Christian faith and others the rules of Christian conduct. The divinity of Jesus Christ, and other truths dear to the heart of the believer, would shine out far more clearly and gloriously after a faithful revision. The strongest and most effective arguments of infidelity and scepticism among the common people are founded upon mistranslations of the words of inspiration.

Similar remarks apply also to the versions in common use throughout the greater part of the European continent and among the descendents of Europeans scattered over the world. These are generally conformed to the English version, or the Latin Vulgate, and almost slavishly copy the errors and imperfections of these versions.

We believe it to be our duty to do all in our power to correct such evils. It is not for us to inquire, how much of God's truth may be concealed from men without material injury to their souls. The infidel distinction between essentials and non-essentials in matters of duty, is not to be found in Scripture. GOD says:

"Ye shall not add to the word that I command you, neither shall ye diminish aught from it." Deut. 4: 2.

"If any man shall add unto these things, God shall add unto him the plagues that are written in this book. And, if any man shall take away from the words of the book of this prophecy, God shall take away his part out of the book of life, and out of the holy city, and from the things which are written in this book." Rev. 22: 18, 19.

Here is no room for the doctrine of EXPEDIENCY, that bane of Christian principle, which withers the energies and neutralizes the influence of so many who profess the name of Christ!

We refer to the Annual Report for the year ending Oct. 3, 1851, for an explanation of all that has been done by the Bible Union, particularly in respect to the revision of the Spanish, the French, and the English Scriptures. We shall probably have a corrected Spanish Testament in circulation within a year. The arrangements for the French are very favorable, but not so mature. In the plan adopted for the English, the following principle is embodied:

> "To give to the ordinary reader, as nearly as possible, the exact meaning of the inspired original, while so far as compatible with this design, the general style and phraseology of the commonly received version are retained." The plan includes the employment of Paedobaptist as well as Baptist scholarship of the highest character. No compromise of the truth in its simplicity, its purity, and its clearness will be made, to gain the cooperation and sanction of any man, or any body of men. But while the principle of the most scrupulous fidelity to God, is inflexibly adhered to, no suitable means will be neglected to bring forth the book with the greatest weight of human authority, which, consistently with that principle, can be secured.

The progress made in the prosecution of this plan, may be understood from the closing paragraphs of a Report made by a Committee from different States at the last Anniversary, Oct. 2, 1851.

"On reviewing all the acts and proceedings of the Board and the Committee on Versions, in relation to the correction of the English Scriptures, your Committee have come to the following conclusions:

1st. That all has been accomplished which could reasonably have been expected, or required, during the brief time that has elapsed since the organization of the American Bible Union.

2d. That the determination of the Greek text, which should constitute the basis of the correction, was a necessary preliminary, to which, the Committee observe with pleasure, much attention, correspondence, and research has been devoted, and they are happy to learn that this part of the enterprise has been satisfactorily accomplished.

3d. That the next important part, was the preparation and maturing of a suitable plan of revision and publication, which should combine in the book the largest amount of intrinsic merit with the greatest share of authority, and in this the Committee regard the Board as having been eminently successful.

4th. That in the prosecution of the plan devised and adopted—the Board have so far matured their measures, and their negotiations with eminent scholars in Great Britain and this country, as to be justified in proceeding to consummate contracts for the performance of the work.

5th. That all the circumstances of the case appear to justify the expectation, that the revision of the New Testament will be completed, and the book be in the course of publication within the next two or three years; and the Committee are of opinion that to attempt to force it through in much less time would be disastrous to its real worth.

The Committee having now completed their report, upon the subject referred to them, beg leave to add that, in view of the large amount of pecuniary means which will be necessarily required for the proper prosecution of the plan adopted by the Board, and the great need of similar aid in the other fields of the Union's labors, they recommend to all who love the truth of God and desire to circulate it in its purity, to contribute zealously and liberally to the funds of the American Bible Union.

The English tongue is more widely spoken than any other. It is the language of commerce, and of missions. The rapidity of its progress and of the races that use it, bids fair to make it the medium of communication over the greater part of the earth. A pure version of the sacred Scriptures in this language, will probably do more good, and exert a more extended influence than in all other languages in the world.

THOS. SWAIN,	A. WHEELOCK,
DAVID E. THOMAS,	SAMUEL ADLAM,
JAMES CHALLEN,	JAMES INGLIS.

The Bible Union has been organized, because no other society sought the objects which it has in view. As no man can be a Christian, who is not willing to obey Christ in all things, so no society can be consistent in principle, which approves of pure versions in one part of the world and not in another. Least of all can a Bible Society justly claim our cooperation which declares that "It is not their province and duty to attempt on their own part, or to procure from others, a revision of the commonly received English version of the Sacred Scriptures" and which binds itself by solemn resolution that "the Society in its issues and circulation of the English Scriptures be restricted to the commonly received version without note or comment;" while it is undeniable that the numerous errors and imperfections of that version have attracted the attention of critics and commentators from the time when it was first published, and their attempted correction constitutes a considerable share of the duty of an intelligent minister in his weekly ministrations. We engage in no warfare with any other institution, and are antagonistic to nothing but error. In the Bible Union we can operate with no restriction upon conscience, and with the full conviction of the approval of Him who directs that His word should be written "very plainly" and that nothing should be added to it or taken from it.

The questions, Christian reader, which we propose for your consideration, are these:

Is it right to continue the publication of known and acknowledged errors as a part of God's word, when you have the power to correct them and to publish the truth?

Can you, consistently with your obligations to Christ, refuse to aid, to the extent of your ability, in removing from his precious word the unauthorized additions of man, which pervert the meaning or obscure the sense?

You acknowledge that the work ought to be done. If the Bible Union does not accomplish it, who will? Shall we be left to work without your assistance? Would you have us do the whole first and then come to you for aid? No, my brother, if the enterprise is worthy, it is your duty to help it NOW. The Lord grant you grace to meet the duty in the spirit of cheerful obedience and to His name be the glory.

Spencer H. Cone, President.

Wm H. Wyckoff, Cor. Secretary.

Notes

Chapter 1. Birth and childhood
1. *Some account of the Life of Spencer Houghton Cone* by his sons Edward W. Cone and Spencer Wallace Cone, New York, 1856, p.12.

Chapter 2. Actor
1. *Life of Spencer Houghton Cone*, p.53.

Chapter 3. Conversion
1. *Life of Spencer Houghton Cone*, pp.86-7.

Chapter 4. Soldier
1.The first battle of Manassas was fought near Bull Run Creek, just southeast of Washington, D. C. Here a group of Federal troops led by General Irvin McDowell, who had gone out against a Confederate army with great confidence, was routed. A kind of picnic atmosphere had at first prevailed before this engagement as many citizens of Washington and surrounding towns had come out to watch. When the men in blue were defeated, they ran helter-skelter over the highway leading to Washington and mingled with many terrified people who were also escaping. This early defeat of the Federal forces produced panic in the nation's capital and caused Lincoln to boost the defences of Washington and rethink his war strategy.
2. *Life of Spencer Houghton Cone*, p.121.
3. While Spencer Cone and his compatriots were in a life and death struggle on land, out in the Baltimore harbour an historic event was unfolding. After

the capital in Washington had been burned, drunken British soldiers were rampaging in Maryland. Dr William Beanes organized a posse to lock up these troublemakers. The British captured him, however, and he was taken onto a ship anchored in the harbour. A Washington lawyer, Francis Scott Key, went on board to try to negotiate the doctor's release. He was held prisoner for ten days and while he was on board he watched the fantastic bombardment of Fort McHenry. At night he could hear the cannons booming out their missiles and he could see them bursting in the air, but he could not tell whether the fort had surrendered. As the morning dawned on 14 September, however, the lawyer's heart leaped for joy, for the American flag was still waving above the beleaguered redoubt. The flag was huge, 30 feet high and 42 feet long. It had been sewn by Mary Pickersgill and her daughter Caroline in 1813, under the orders of Lt. Col. George Armistead. When Key saw the American flag had survived the terrific bombardment of the English warships, he was inspired to write the now famous words, 'O, say can you see, by the dawns, early light...' etc. This song is now the national anthem of America.

Chapter 5. First preaching

1. *Life of Spencer Houghton Cone*, pp.134-5.

2. *Ibid.*, pp.135-6.

3. Obadiah Brown (1779-1852) was a native of New Jersey and originally a Presbyterian, but during his twenties he espoused Baptist views and studied under Rev. W. Van Horn of Scotch Plains, NJ. After pursuing a teaching career for several years he was ordained to the ministry and preached for a while at Salem, NJ. He became pastor of the Baptist church in Washington in 1807, a position he held for forty-three years. He served as chaplain to Congress on numerous occasions, was a member of the board of trustees of Columbia College, and was associated with Luther Rice and others who organized the Baptist General Convention, the first national Baptist organization in America. He had a vigorous mind and was a very effective preacher. (See Cathcart's *Baptist Encyclopedia*).

4. Cited in his biography. Cone's elation at having won a soul to Christ was taken by his biographers from an 1844 'Sermon to the Young'.

Chapter 6. Alexandria pastorate

1. 'The Funeral Sermon on the Death of Rev. Spencer Houghton Cone, D.D.',
preached by the Rev. Thomas Armitage, D.D., Saturday Afternoon, 16
September 1855 (New York, 1855), pp.38-9.
2. *Life of Spencer Houghton Cone*, p.150.
3. *Ibid.*, p.249.

Chapter 7. The spirit of mission

1. *Life of Spencer Houghton Cone*, p.168.
2. *Ibid.*, p.176.
3. *Ibid.*, p.180.
4. *Ibid.*, pp.182-3.
5. *Ibid.*, p.183.
6. *Ibid.*, pp.183-4.
7. These documents were reprinted by W. J. Berry in a booklet entitled *The
Kehukee Declaration and Black Rock Address, with Other Writings Relative
to the Baptist Separation between 1825-1840,* edited by Gilbert Beebe
(Primitive Publications, Elon College, North Carolina n.d.)
8. *Life of Spencer Cone*, p.181.

Chapter 8. New York City

1. The evangelical church of this era, including Baptists had no qualms about
bringing people of all races into their fellowship. The painful divisions attending
the Civil War changed this open, Christ-like attitude and resulted in the
shameful racial prejudices which still linger in America today. Inclusion,
regrettably, did not mean equality even then, however, for often the black
believers were required to sit in a different part of the church.
2. *The Life of Spencer Houghton Cone*, p.200.
3. *Ibid.*, p.200.
4. *Ibid.*, p.201.
5. One cannot help but be impressed by the contrast between the careful and
tender spirit in which these negotiations were going on and the tumultuous
and hostile attitudes that often prevail when pastoral relationships are broken
up in many Baptist churches today. The average Baptist pastor today lasts

for only about two years, and more often than not, it seems, the biblical model of a loving relationship between the spiritual shepherd and his sheep seems all too often to be missing. This writer has heard numerous cases in which even common courtesies, not to mention biblical patterns for settling disputes, are set aside when preachers are dismissed. The causes for such a fairly general deterioration of pastoral relations in contemporary society, and a need for a proper remedy, should be a major topic for study and reflection, especially among our Baptist churches where no presiding Bishop or regional body has full authority for resolving conflict.

6. *Ibid.*, pp.208-9.
7. *Ibid.*, p.210.
8. *Ibid.*, p.210.

Chapter 9. Shocks in the family circle
1. *Life of Spencer Houghton Cone*, pp.226-7.
2. *Ibid.*, pp.216-17.

Chapter 10. Expanding Horizons
1. *Life of Spencer Houghton Cone*, p.230.
2. *Ibid.*, p.231.
3. *Ibid.*, p.248.

Chapter 11. Choosing for change
1. *Life of Spencer Houghton Cone*, p.253.
2. *Ibid.*, p.260.
3. *Ibid.*, pp.260-1.
4. *Ibid.*, p.262-3.
5. *Ibid.*, p.264.
6. *Ibid.*, p.264.
7. *Ibid.*, pp.264-5.

Chapter 12. First Baptist Church
1. Sprague W., *Annals of the American Baptist Pulpit*, New York, 1860, p.62.

2. The author, when a child, attended at one time with his father a church of the old order of Regular Baptists which followed this custom. The method was for a reader or leader to recite a line and the congregation would sing in response, with the correct intonation. I cannot refrain from telling a story that was often related among those of this communion, including my father, with a round of hearty laugher. It is said that once a brother was leading the church in singing the old hymn attributed to Cenneck, which begins with 'Jesus my all to heaven is gone'. He recited these lines, and the congregation as usual sang them in response. But then the reader was distracted as he looked out the window, and he inserted quite unconsciously the exclamation, 'Here comes a horse with a side saddle on,' which a few in the crowd faithful sang out. Then looking again at his little hymnal he read, 'His track I'll see and I'll pursue,' which the congregation dutifully repeated. Then looking out the window again he said, 'Well, I'll be dogged, he broke it smack into,' which a few sleepy worshippers, incredibly, sang out. Whether this story is apocryphal or authentic I cannot tell, but it was often told in the circles of the Primitive Baptists. This song is number 41 in the old 'Sweet Songster' as it is called, the Primitive Baptist Hymn Book which I inherited from my father.

3. *Life of Spencer Houghton Cone*, p.270.

Chapter 13. Isaac McCoy

1. As cited in *Life of Spencer Houghton Cone*, p.31. Stow is described in the 1881 Baptist Encyclopedia as 'one of the most eloquent and successful ministers' of his denomination. He was born in Hew Hampshire but held pastorates primarily in Massachusetts. He pastored the Baldwin Place Church from 1832 till 1848 during which time he saw many people converted. A powerful revival occurred in 1838 during which over 500 people joined the church on a profession of faith. This writer was fortunate enough to find many years ago a copy of *The Psalmist, a New Collection of Hymns for the Use of Baptist Churches*, which he edited, along with the S. F. Smith. The latter is the author of the patriotic hymn, 'My Country Tis of Thee.' This hymn book, consisting of over 1200 hymns (no music is included), is a treasury of outstanding, theologically sound poetry which was used by godly Baptists of another day.

2. *Life of Spencer Houghton Cone*, p.308.

3. Cited in John T. *Christian's History of the Baptists*, vol. II, p.414.

4. *Life of Spencer Houghton Cone*, p.285.

5. *Ibid.*, p.284.

6. *Ibid.*, p.294.

7. *Ibid.*, p.283.

Chapter 14. The great division

1. Torbet, Robert G., *A History of the Baptists*, p.291. Torbet clearly summarizes in short compass the background and development of the division of Northern and Southern Baptists. This volume is the primary source for the information on this subject here.

2. *Ibid.*, p.291.

3. *Life of Spencer Houghton Cone*, p.278.

Chapter 15. The Bible translation controversy

1. *History of the Baptists*, p.904.

2. *Life of Spencer Houghton Cone*, p.336.

3. In recent years many evangelical Christians, for the most part associated with the 'Christian Right' have repudiated the concept of the separation of church and state, on the grounds that a certain belief in the Bible and Christ inheres in the American democracy. Even some Baptists have joined in this crusade. In this regard they have departed from the traditional views of their forefathers in earlier days of our republic. Were Spencer Cone and men of his ilk living today, they would have been much more afraid of a dominant, powerful church in collusion with the secular government than they would 'secular humanism' latent in public institutions.

4. So James David Knowles, a teacher at Newton Theological Institution, reported later, as cited in Armitage, p.898.

Chapter 16. A confessional faith

1. *History of the Baptists*, p.903.

2. *The Commonly Received Version of the Bible,* p.1.

3. Printed in a pamphlet entitled 'Principles and Intentions of the American Bible Union'.

4. *Life of Spencer Houghton Cone*, p.274.

5. See this confession of faith in its entirely in the appendix. This statement of faith is admirable for its careful and close usage of biblical language, and avoids some of the technical language and controversial terminology which other Baptist confessions have used, often adapted from Paedobaptist documents.

Chapter 17. A powerful pen

1. 'Minutes of the Fifty-Sixth Anniversary of the New-York Baptist Association', New York, 1846, pp.18-19.

2. In the mid-1990s under the wise and forceful leadership of Dr R. Albert Mohler, Jr., the Southern Baptist Seminary in Louisville has reaffirmed its theological stance as outlined in the Abstract of Principles, which was drawn up at the very time of its inauguration. This confession affirms essentially the view espoused by Spencer Cone. News of this reaffirmation has produced a vehement negative reaction on the part of many Baptist leaders in Kentucky who have been trained in earlier days when Calvinism was considered an ancient heresy long since expunged from the churches.

3. 'The Funeral Sermon on the Death of Rev. Spencer Houghton Cone, D.D', New York, 1855, p.33.

4. *Ibid.*, pp.34-5.

5. 'The Restoration of the Jews', A Circular Letter of the New York Baptist Association, 1844, in the American Baptist Historical Society archives, Rochester, NY, p.1.

6. *Ibid.*, pp.5-6.

7. *Ibid.*, p.7.

Chapter 18. Counselling young ministers

1. *Life of Spencer Houghton Cone*, pp.444-5.

2. *Ibid.*, pp.420,432.

3. *Ibid.*, p.281.

4. *Ibid.*, p.423.

5. *Ibid.*, p.426.

6. *Ibid.*, pp.426-7.

7. *Ibid.*, p.444.

222218A pastor in New York

8. *Ibid.*, p.425.

9. *Ibid.*, p.425.

10. *Ibid.*, p.424.

11. *Ibid.*, pp.417-18.

12. *Ibid.*, pp. 418-19.

Chapter 19. Sally's homegoing

1. *Life of Spencer Houghton Cone*, p.451.

2. *Ibid.*, p.452.

3. *Ibid.*, pp.452-3.

4. *Ibid.*, p.457.

5. *Ibid.*, p.457.

6. From the web site of Washington Township, Long Valley, New Jersey.

7. *Life of Cone*, p.463.

8. *Ibid.*, pp.466-7.

Chapter 20. Dying on the field of battle

1. In 1846 a gentleman, about Cone's own age, who had been active as a home missionary, signified his wish not to be re-elected to his office because of being advanced in years. A mutual friend suggested to Spencer Cone that the missionary society pass a resolution commending this man for his service and expressing regret at his retirement. Cone could see no need for such a commendation, and suggested rather that a resolution be passed urging the brother to continue on in his work. 'If you offer a resolution that brother _____ be desired to continue in the work till the Lord calls him home,' he replied, 'I will second it and make a speech. I have enlisted for life; I intend to die with the harness on.' Thus did Cone express his opinion of the idea of an able-bodied man retiring from the field of divine service.

2. 'The Funeral Sermon of Rev. Spencer Houghton Cone, D.D.', New York, 1855, p.v.

3. *The New Park Street Pulpit*, 1856, Alabaster and Passmore, London, p.v.

Chapter 21. The legacy of Spencer Houghton Cone

1. His friend J. L. Dagg communicated to him shortly before he died, and in a letter he said to the theologian, 'You ask if my views have changed with reference to what are usually known as "the doctrines of grace". Not a jot. The 10th of John, and 8th of Romans, and 1st and 2nd of Ephesians are dear to me as ever. Grace reigning through righteousness unto eternal life by Jesus Christ our Lord, is the only plan by which sinners can be saved. If I am not complete in Christ, I have no hope of ever entering into the mansions of bliss. But I hear him say, "because I live ye shall live also," and then I reply with holy boldness,"Surely I shall dwell in the house of the Lord for ever!"' (*Life of Spencer Houghton Cone*, p. 408).

Index